18 Management Competencies
Business Professionals Cannot Ignore!

18 Management Competencies
Business Professionals Cannot Ignore!

Saugata Mitra
Seema Bangia
Jayati Mitra

STERLING PUBLISHERS PRIVATE LIMITED

STERLING PUBLISHERS PRIVATE LIMITED
A-59, Okhla Industrial Area, Phase-II,
New Delhi-110020.
Tel: 26387070, 26386209; Fax: 91-11-26383788
E-mail: sterlingpublishers@airtelmail.in
ghai@nde.vsnl.net.in
www.sterlingpublishers.com

18 Management Competencies
Business Professionals Cannot Ignore!
© 2008, *Saugata Mitra*
ISBN 978-81-207-3924-6

All rights are reserved. No part of this publication may be reproduced, stored in a retrieval system or transmitted, in any form or by any means, mechanical, photocopying, recording or otherwise, without prior written permission of the original publisher.

Printed and Published by Sterling Publishers Pvt. Ltd., New Delhi-110 020.

Preface

In a world of complexity, the use of complex thoughts, complex words and terminology for simple things in everyday life are valued and used in one-to-one interactions, conferences, classrooms and boardrooms to create awe amongst the audience. The audience comes back carrying no new learning but a short-lived memory of the speakers' choice of words and terminology.

However, if we look back, we recall some people who have broken through these complexities and have communicated even complex thoughts in a simple language which we understand. Those are the lessons that we carry and use in our daily life even today.

The infant's initial explorations in the world of physical senses are guided by its mother. She is often the first person who breaks the complex world and takes her child on the path of learning. Alphabets and numbers constitute some of the most complex symbols, but the child learns them, *never* to forget them. The fact of the matter is that we only carry with us 30% of the learning from our academic career and that 30% is the part that has been separated from complexities and communicated in the language we understand; 70% remains scattered and disconnected information which falls by the wayside.

18 Management Competencies: Business Professionals Cannot Ignore! is a book written by management professionals for easy understanding and use by students and practitioners of Business and Management. It is not an academic treatise. The purpose of the book is to communicate the DNA of human performance in a language which is easily understood.

Human Resource has been identified as the only living resource without which none of the other resources can move to deliver the business outcomes. Amongst the many factors impacting human performance, competency has been identified for in-depth study. A brief introduction of the origin and initial development of this much debated but elusive concept has been provided for the benefit of readers.

In a sense, the main inspiration for putting together this work came from our professional experience of working with large organisations competing to acquire and retain the best talent in the country. This gave us insight into the core of HR issues and an understanding of the new challenges being faced by HR professionals in a rapidly changing business environment. We found the area of competencies particularly fascinating and challenging and decided to address the basic concerns of management professionals in terms of competencies needed at different levels.

We have tried to identify specific competencies without which business results are not possible and what these mean in real terms at different levels of management. One important aspect of the competency has been illustrated in a lighter vein for easy understanding and recall. These again capture simple real-life situations. The micro case studies attempt to show how successful people have demonstrated a specific competency in real life. These are anecdotal case studies and do not imply that a particular business leader stands for a specific competency. In fact, the business leaders featured would have most, if not all, the competencies in some measure to be where they are today.

It is felt that business professionals and HR practitioners would benefit immensely by investing a few hours in this book and improving their ability to handle real-life situations.

March 2008 *Saugata Mitra*
New Delhi

Acknowledgements

A work of this nature cannot be conceived, drafted and published without the direct or indirect inputs of a large number of people and institutions. It may just not be possible to name everyone in this limited space; however, we would first like to thank Abbscissa Human Resource Consulting, a leading Consulting company based in New Delhi for promoting the whole project and providing financial support for research and editorial work until the document was ready for publishing. Abbscissa has been in the forefront of Talent & Competency Management for a number of Fortune 500 companies and they did see a gap and a need for such a book.

As regards the micro case studies, we are thankful to ICMR Center for Management Research, Hyderabad, and McGraw Hill Education (India), Noida U.P. for permission to use material from their works. The specific cases from each of these institutions have been identified with an appropriate footnote.

We are also grateful to our editor Tapan K. Ghosh who gave inputs to make the work reader friendly, visualised the illustrations and had them executed by A.V. Prasanth, a talented young cartoonist and painter. Last, but not the least, our grateful thanks to S.K Ghai of Sterling Publishers who found merit in this effort and decided to go ahead with its publication immediately.

The authors

Contents

Preface	v
Acknowledgements	vii

PART 1

■ Introduction	3
■ Competency: Definition and History	10

PART 2: KEY COMPETENCIES

Interpersonal Skills

1. Communication:
   - **Definition and Proficiency levels** — 19
   - **Case studies:**
     - Enhancing the Appeal of Titan — 23
     - Boundaryless Behaviour – A Lesson from GE — 25
     - Bhavarlal Jain: Courageous Communicator — 26
     - Hewlett and Packard: The Open-Door Policy — 29
2. Influence and Negotiations
   - **Definition and Proficiency levels** — 31
   - **Case studies:**
     - Averting Strike at Bangalore — 35
     - E. Sreedharan: Iconic Project Manager — 37
     - Philips India: To Sell or Not? — 39
3. Building Relationships
   - **Definition and Proficiency levels** — 40
   - **Case studies:**
     - Biocon Leader – Kiran Mazumdar — 45
     - HR Visionary – Narayana Murthy — 46
     - B. M. Munjal: The Hero Group — 48

People Development

1. Teamwork
   - **Definition and Proficiency levels**   53
   - **Case studies:**
     - The Dabbawalas of Mumbai   57
     - K. M. Birla: Visionary Team Builder   59
     - Infosys – Building Teams on Core Values   60
2. Leadership
   - **Definition and Proficiency levels**   63
   - **Case studies:**
     - Jack Welch: The Making of a CEO   67
     - Mukesh Ambani: Chasing New Frontiers   70
     - Shahnaz Husain: Pioneer and Leader   73
3. Building Capabilities
   - **Definition and Proficiency levels**   75
   - **Case studies:**
     - Infosys – Inspiring a New Generation of Leaders   79
     - The Taj's People's Philosophy   81
     - Pramod Chaudhari: Hands-on Learning   83

Work Effectiveness

1. Analytical Skills
   - **Definition and Proficiency levels**   86
   - **Case studies:**
     - Raghunath Mashelkar: A Leader and Scientist   90
     - The Case of AMWAY   91
     - Verghese Kurien: Strategic Leadership   93
2. Decision Making
   - **Definition and Proficiency levels**   96
   - **Case studies:**
     - Vision Behind Small Car – Nano   100
     - Naveen Jindal: Seeing the Bigger Picture   102
     - Sunil Mittal: Business Focus par Excellence   104

Contents

3. Planning and Organising
   - **Definition and Proficiency levels** — 107
   - **Case studies**:
     - The GE Workout – The Bottom-up Approach — 111
     - The Frooti Re-launch — 112

Achieving Business Results

1. Business Focus
   - **Definition and Proficiency levels** — 115
   - **Case studies**:
     - Ford Motor Company – Jacques Nasser — 119
     - Humayun Dhanrajgir: Power of Persuasion — 120
     - Dhirubhai Ambani: Self-made Business Icon — 122
2. Cost and Profit Management
   - **Definition and Proficiency levels** — 124
   - **Case studies**:
     - Telco Turnaround – Bold and Persistent — 128
     - Nissan Turnaround Story — 130
     - Gillette's Restructuring in India — 133
3. Service Focus
   - **Definition and Proficiency levels** — 136
   - **Case studies**:
     - Bharat Petroleum Corporation Ltd., (BPCL) — 140
     - Jack Welch & GE – Meeting Customer Demands — 141
     - Deepak Parekh & HDFC's Customer Focus — 143

Professional Improvement

1. Managing Changing Environment
   - **Definition and Proficiency levels** — 147
   - **Case studies**:
     - K. V. Kamath: Change Management at ICICI — 151
     - Jagdish Khattar: Re-packaging Maruti — 154
     - K. M. Birla's Philosophy of Change — 156

2. Continuous Improvement/Innovation
   - **Definition and Proficiency levels**   159
   - **Case studies:**
     - Innovation at Wipro   163
     - Lessons from NOKIA   165
     - Recruitment – The CISCO Way   166
3. Personal Responsibility
   - **Definition and Proficiency levels**   169
   - **Case studies:**
     - Responsibility to Shareholders – Dhirubhai Way   173
     - Aditya Vikram Birla: Investing in Quality   175
4. Technical Skills
   - **Definition and Proficiency levels**   177
   - **Case studies:**
     - Sony Corporation – Managing a Global Corporation   181
     - Bill Gates: His Technical Leadership   184
5. Initiative and Proactivity
   - **Definition and Proficiency levels**   188
   - **Case studies:**
     - Environmental Hero – Tulsi Kanti   192
     - Deepak Puri: The Moser Baer Story   194
     - Azim Hasham Premji: Wipro's Visionary Leader   196

Competencies for CEOs

- Intellectual Qualities   198
- Adaptable Qualities   200
- Pragmatic Qualities   201
- Achievement-Oriented Qualities   202

References   205

PART ONE

- **INTRODUCTION**
- **COMPETENCY: DEFINITION AND HISTORY**

Introduction

The Common Language of World Human Organisations – The Universal Law

All human organisations of the world evolve, develop and sustain with an objective to satisfy some human need. The objective is generally unifocal, common and universal in nature; the organisation revolves around that objective which becomes the common language of that organisation. Any deviation from the common language leads to suffering and sorrow for the human society at large. Some simple examples of different kinds of human organisations are given in the table below:

Organisations	The Common Universal language	Deviation from the Common Universal language	Human Suffering	Result
Political	Good governance	Corrupt, inefficient	Stifles the aspiration and growth of the citizen	Change of government
Economic	Creating wealth for the nation and value to the share holders	Unviable, sick and closure	Revenue loss to the nation and unemployment	Change of management
Religious	Universal love and human values	Fundamentalism	Terrorism	Banned, outlawed and change of leadership.
Social	Service to mankind	Corrupt, inefficient	Inhumanity	Change of leadership

Human society across the world has created organisations for their needs. The deliverables are crystal clear, common and universal in nature. They entrust the deliverables to a set of people in various time intervals and they are intolerant to any deviation from the common universal language of these human organisations. We have observed, across these organisations – political, economic, religious and social – the common universal language has not seen any change from time immemorial; though with time there has been change in the structure but never the common language. On the other hand, we have seen, whenever and whoever has deviated from the common language, human society has replaced these set of people with others who abide by the common universal language.

Common Language of Business – The Universal Law

In simple terms, any economic enterprise whether small or among the Fortune 500s, is constituted of several elements: materials, machines, money, market and man, or the five **M's** (Fig.1). All these elements or resources have one purpose or path. They must lead to **surplus profit** or **value** for the shareholders or investors. In other words, after all the expenses and taxes have been paid, some surplus in terms of monetary benefit must accrue to the entrepreneurs and the investors. This is the universal law of business, be it street vendors , small businesses or large transnational organisations and it is global for everyone in the platform of business.

But more than anything else it is **people,** the second part of the universal law that is critical to any enterprise. In today's competitive world the resources of any enterprise are handled by professionals. These professionals, belonging to different specialisations together move the business effectively and efficiently towards the common language of business and make it worthwhile for the entrepreneurs to continue with the enterprise. The **human resource** of a business house is perhaps its most valuable asset, as it is the only living organism in the whole superstructure which drives, manages and develops the other resources. No other resource

Introduction

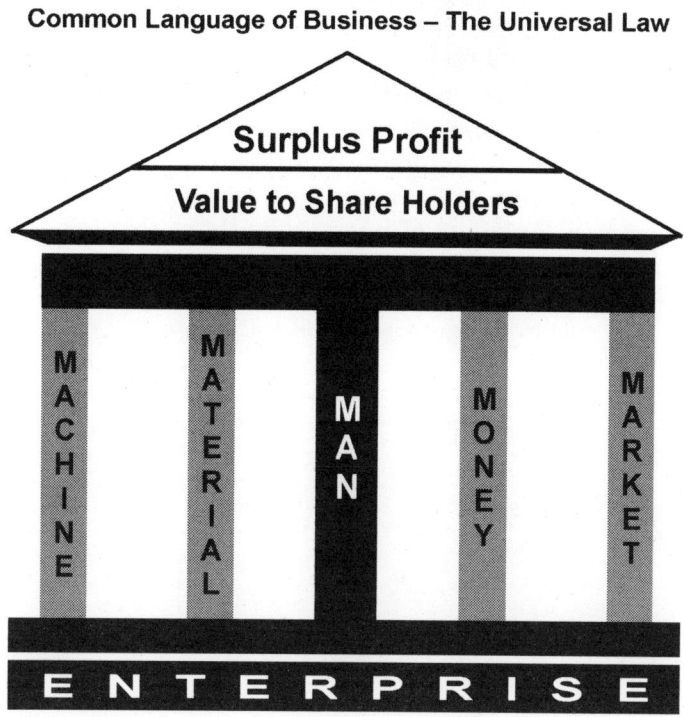

Fig. 1

can function without this resource. In other words, the professionals manage the existing assets and create new ones for the business. Without a good team of professionals, no enterprise would find it easy to create value for the share holders and, in fact, may go out of business. No wonder then that successful entrepreneurs and business houses all over the world concentrate their energies on building a strong and efficient human resource (HR) base in terms of philosophy, policy and practices. It is worthwhile recalling Narayana Murthy's statement when Infosys had not yet become the IT giant it is now: "My real assets come to office at 8 a.m. each morning and leave by 6.30 p.m. each evening. It is them I worry about everyday." In fact, the Indian business world has so much to learn from Murthy, who showed extraordinary vision in finding the best people, getting the best out of them and then retaining them.

The DNA of the Super Resource – Human Resource

Human Resource is the mother of all resources; the one animate resource without which no inanimate resource can move to achieve the objectives of an economic enterprise. Removing this resource from an economic enterprise will lead to the stoppage of the lifeline of an economic enterprise. In fact, all other resources cannot and will not move towards the common language of business without this one super resource – Human Resource (Fig.2).

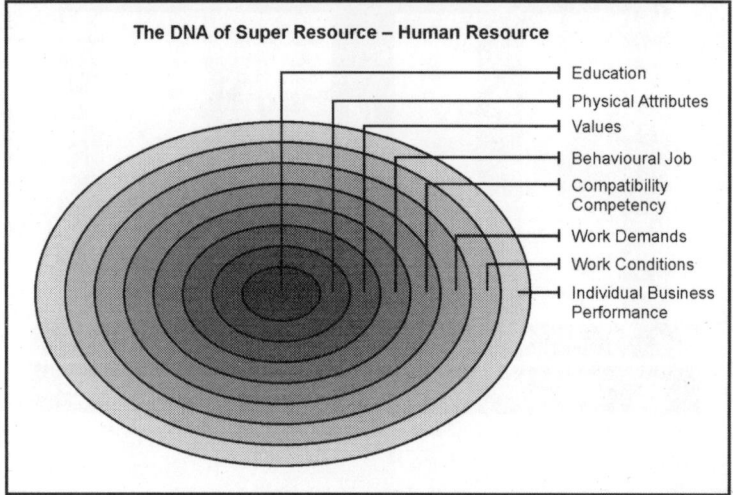

Fig. 2

The quality of the business professional is critical to the success of any economic venture. Hence, one needs to dissect, analyze and understand the core components which makes a business professional achieve the objectives or the common language of business.

The Basic Components for a Job

Education:

This refers to the information and knowledge acquired for preparing oneself intellectually for a mature life, and in particular for a profession. In modern times, this formal imparting of education is done through the platform of schools, colleges and universities, followed by rigorous testing, certification and grant of various degrees.

Introduction

Hence, in the corporate world, we have a set educational requirement for various job categories. Broadly these are:

Managerial – MBA, CA, CS, etc.
Technical – B.Tech, M.Tech, etc.
Tertiary – B.A., B.Com, M.A., M.Com, M.Sc., etc.

Physical Attributes:

Inherent physical qualities are required for doing any kind of job. Generally, every job requires people with good physical health and a sound mind; however, some jobs require special physical attributes.

Job	*Physical Attributes*
Soldier	Muscle and fitness
Teaching	Voice
Basketball Player	Height
Pilot	Eyesight

Values:

There are dos and don'ts of any particular civilised society, institutionalised over a period of time. Every economic enterprise aspires for potential candidates with strong values. Some of them are: honesty, integrity, commitment, fairness, goodness, courtesy, truthfulness, collaboration, cooperation, loyalty, reliability and harmony.

Business results when a number of managerial and environmental factors work in a judicious combination with the core or basic components as is shown below (Fig.3).

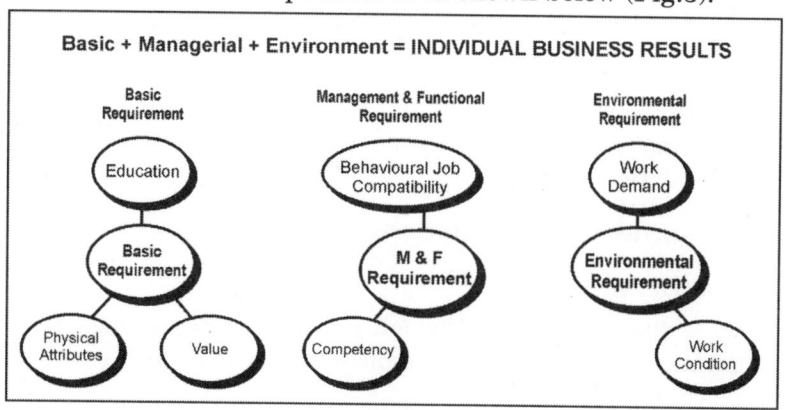

Fig. 3

Management and Functional Components for a Job

Behavioural Job Compatibility:

There are certain behavioural requirements of a job. The behaviour of a person is an index of some of the questions like:
- What are his working strengths and limitations?
- Is he a self-starter?
- How does he communicate?
- What motivates him?

The behavioural assessment of a person helps an organisation to assess his work style. The behavioural requirement of a particular role can be matched with the person's behaviour to assess how well that person fits into that role i.e.,
- A Sales Person – High on Influencing Skills
- A Finance Professional – High on Compliance
- An Engineer – High on Steadiness and Compliance
- A Police Officer – High on Dominance.

Competency:

The most accepted definition by human resource professionals: Competencies are what the performer has and uses for the performance of his job. It can be defined as:
– A combination of skills, knowledge and attitude that affects a major part of the job.
– Co-relates with performance on the job.
– Can be measured against well-accepted standards.
– Can be improved through training and development.

Examples – Leadership; building relationships; planning and organizing; communication; initiative; and proactive thinking and analytical skills.

Environmental Components for a Job

Work Demands:

This is basically what the job performers need from the organisation, in the form of tools and essential resources to perform the job successfully.

Introduction

Job	Tools
Surgeon	Operation Theatre
News Reader	News Room
S/w Programmer	Computer with required software

Work Conditions:

This is basically what the performer receives for the job he is performing, which in human resource terminology is defined as work environment, compensation, development, growth, welfare, etc. In simple words, what does he get in return for the job executed and is it comparable with others? Does the return make one motivated enough for an effective performance? The challenge for the HR professionals throughout the world is innovating ways and new methods for attracting, developing, engaging and retaining human resource or talent.

2

Competency: Definition and History

In the introduction chapter we talked about the DNA of human resource and said that the individual's business performance is dependent on various components – Basic, Management, and Environmental. Since the book is primarily focused on management and functional requirements for the job, we would be focusing on **competencies**.

A. What Competency is Not

It may be worthwhile to identify and understand what is *not competency,* to arrive at a better understanding of what is competency. Though there is a very thin line between traits, talent and competency, the following are *not* competencies:

1. An ability which is a natural talent with which we can do without prior formal training for instance – handling small items, walking, talking, dancing, singing, etc.
2. A capability which is built-in as physical traits in a person for instance – height, weight, etc.
3. Personality traits which are again in-built or inherent in a person for instance – loyalty, honesty, openness, etc.
4. Motivational attitude i.e., characteristics which are motives and intentions. One can have, for instance – ambition, self-confidence, etc.

Profession	What competency Is not.........	Category	Competency
Soldier	Muscle	Physical Attribute	Determination
Teacher	Voice	Physical Attribute	Interpersonal skills
Salesman	Highest Sales	Result	Communication
Pediatrician	Liking for Children	Trait/Character	Patience

B. Definition of Competency

The most widely accepted definition accepted by HR professionals, evolved from the suggestions from human resource experts attending a conference on competencies in Johannesburg in 1995. Essentially this means:

1. A combination of skills, knowledge and attitude that affects a major part of one's job.
2. Correlates with performance on the job.
3. Can be measured against well-accepted standards.
4. Can be improved through training and development (Parry, 1996)

C. The Test of Competency – What is Competency

In determining **what is and is not** a competency, based on the above definition, anything that goes through the scanner with its four levels of filtering is a competency (see Fig.4).

D. Job Evaluation, Job Levels, Competency and Proficiency Level

Job evaluation is a systematic process for defining the relative worth or size of jobs within an organisation in order to establish internal relativities and provide the basis for designing an organisational structure, job level structure, grade and pay structure. Hence, in any organisation you have a typical level termed as Senior Management, Middle Management and Junior Management.

For each level of management the following are defined:

(1) The Business Deliverables. (2) The competencies along with the proficiency level required for the level. (3) The reward in terms of the compensation and other motivators.

In this book the competencies are defined along with the proficiency levels required for the various levels of management. Proficiency Level C, the highest and advanced level has been defined for the senior management; Proficiency Level B, the intermediary level has been defined for mid-management; and proficiency Level A, the rudimentary level, for the junior management.

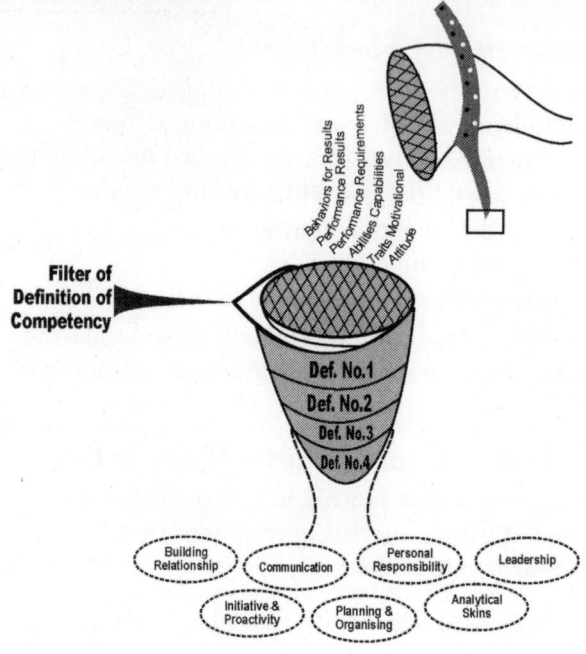

Fig. 4

However, this does not entail that a senior management person should not have the level B or A proficiencies.

E. Origin of Competency as a Concept; Brief History

Just to recapitulate, competencies can, at its simplest, be seen as general descriptions of the **abilities** necessary to perform successfully in specific areas. Competency profiles synthesize *skills, knowledge, attributes and values* and express performance requirements in behavioural terms.

Despite a growing interest in competency among managers and human resource professionals in recent years, the modern competency movement in industrial-organisational psychology actually dates back to the mid fifties and early seventies.

In this regard, John Flanagan's work (1954) and David McClelland's studies (in 1970s) might be cited as two landmark efforts that originally conceived and developed the concept of competency.

The Work of John Flanagan

John Flanagan published a seminal work in 1954 and established the Critical Incidents Technique, which became a precursor to the key methodology used in rigorous competency studies. Based on studies of performances of U.S. Air Force pilots, Flanagan concluded that "the principle objective of job-analysis procedures should be the determination of critical requirements. These requirements include those which have been demonstrated to have made the difference, between success and failure in carrying out an important part of the job assigned in a significant number of instances". From here, Critical Incidents Technique was originally conceived as a process.

Critical Incidents Technique came to be understood as a set of procedures for systematically identifying behaviours that contribute to success or failure of individuals or organisations in specific situations.

Flanagan's work, while not strictly about competencies, was important because it laid the foundation for a new approach to examining what people do. In a later form, the critical incidents technique would resurface to focus around significant behavioural events that distinguish between exemplary and fully successful achievers or performers. It was Flanagan's critical incidents technique that sixteen years later inspired David McClelland to come up with and develop the term "competency".

David McClelland's thinking on the subject was originally driven by researchers who were uneasy and dissatisfied with the reliability and thus the value of testing personality traits in predicting job performance. For instance, Ghiselli (1966) and Mischel (1968) found that testable personality traits had little correlation with job performance and consequently research on these variables was of questionable value.

Around the same time, an increasing number of studies published demonstrated that traditional academic aptitude and knowledge content tests as well as school grades and credentials did not predict job performance; moreover, these were often biased against women and people from the lower socio-economic strata.

McClelland (1973) then conducted an intensive research programme in order to identify "competency" variables which *did predict* job performance and which were not influenced by sex or socioeconomic factors. Competencies as reliable indicators thus were based on some principles.

The most important of these principles were:

- Use of **criterion sample**: compare people who are clearly successful in jobs with less successful persons to identify those characteristics with success
- Identification of **operant thoughts (knowledge) and behaviours** causally related to these successful outcomes. That is, competency measures should involve open-ended situations in which the individual has to generate behaviour.

By using Flanagan's critical incident method and an intensive method known as behavioural event interview (BEI) to distinguish successful and unsuccessful performers, McClelland attempted to identify characteristics which differed between the two sample groups in terms of behaviour shown by superior performers as compared to average performers.

The essence of McClelland's radical departure in approach to job analysis is that where traditional job analysis *looked at elements of the jobs* or its essential nature, competency assessment studied *the people who do the job well*, and defined *the job in terms of the characteristics and behaviours of these people*.

Subsequently, interest increased in the development of workable models on competency which could be applied across diverse businesses and professions. In the United States, Richard Boyatzis wrote the first empirically-based and fully researched book on competency model developments. It was following the work of Boyatzis that job competency came to be widely understood to mean an underlying characteristic of a person that results in or causes superior or effective performance. Boyatzis was explicit in describing the importance of clearly-defined competency as reflected in specific behaviour and clearly defined performance outcomes when he emphasised that "specific actions cause or lead to the specified results. Certain characteristics or abilities of the person enable him or her to demonstrate the appropriate specific actions" (Boyatzis, 1982, p.12).

As the pioneer of competency modeling in the United States, Boyatzis grounded competency interventions on documented behavioural indicators that caused or influenced effective job performance. Boyatzis, like Flanagan, stressed the importance of systematic analysis in collecting and analyzing examples of the actual performance of individuals doing the work. The method for documenting the actual performance was through the behavioural event interview. This was an intensive face-to-face interview that involved soliciting critical incidents from performers and documenting what the performers were thinking and doing during the incidents.

In the Indian context, it is only after the process of liberalisation began in the early nineties that the importance of human resource management became obvious to the business world. Earlier HR functions were seen in a limited way, but things changed when the need to compete in the global market also meant the necessity to recruit and retain the best talent in various fields. Today, even HR managers can aspire to take over the top executive positions in the company. Understanding of the critical role of HR has indeed come a long way.

Part Two

Key Competencies

Proficiencies at different management levels

Level-C: senior management
Level-B: middle management
Level-A: junior management

Interpersonal Skills

1. Communication

"I am here to tell you what I told you in the last meeting. You recall I said that the new business plan will be announced shortly!"

Communication is a process that involves both the sender of the message and the receiver. This process so often leaves room for error, with messages often misinterpreted by one or more of the parties involved. This causes unnecessary confusion and can be counter productive. In fact, a message is successful when both the sender and the receiver perceive and understand it in the same way.

Communication here refers to the process that facilitates sharing of information and ideas across the organisation. No organisation can survive without effective communication, both internal and external. You need communication for everything. You communicate to request, to inform, even to persuade. Communication stimulates others to take action and gives direction to people for achievement of set goals.

With this competency:

One shares and receives information, including views, facts and feelings; communicates clearly and succinctly, checking for understanding and encouraging an open, two-way discussion; identifies appropriate people (internally and externally) to communicate with and tailors the message to their needs.

LEVELS OF PROFICIENCY

Proficiency Level C

"He likes to give short confidential notes to the employees himself. What a leader!!"

- Ensures formal and informal channels are established between different groups to keep every one up to date.
- Speaks and communicates to difficult audiences, moving among a variety of cultural contexts and languages.
- Speaks clearly and succinctly.
- Demonstrates originality and flexibility of communication.
- Identifies communication needs across the organisation and to customers.
- Prepared to contribute to discussions.
- Clear, concise and well-structured written and graphical communication.

"Think like a wise man but communicate in the language of the people."
– *William Butler Yeats (1865 - 1939)*

"We are cups, constantly and quietly being filled. The trick is, knowing how to tip ourselves over and let the beautiful stuff out."
– *Ray Bradbury*

"The way we communicate with others and with ourselves ultimately determines the quality of our lives."
– *Anthony*

Communication

Proficiency Level B

"Oops!! That must have hurt. He said he would show us how to strike when the iron was hot!!!"

- Uses a variety of routes to get the message across.
- Documents decisions.
- Takes clear and well-structured notes.
- Identifies and keeps appropriate people at all levels informed (internal/external)
- Tailors amount and style of communication to audience e.g., summarises key points for directors, supplies exhaustive data and facts for engineers.
- Asks probing questions to identify and understand differences of view.
- Explains technical information to non-specialists without using jargon.
- Makes use of timely and consistent communication.
- Utilises technology to communicate effectively.

"To effectively communicate, we must realise that we are all different in the way we perceive the world and use this understanding as a guide to our communication with others."
— *Anthony Robbins*

"Start with good people, lay out the rules, communicate with your employees, motivate them and reward them. If you do all those things effectively, you can't miss."
— *Lee Iacocca*

"Kind words can be short and easy to speak, but their echoes are truly endless."
— *Mother Teresa*

Proficiency Level A

"Shshh! Just pass on the message. We are getting a good bonus this year!"

- Uses the most appropriate communication channel e.g., e-mail, telephone, face to face.
- Takes time to ensure that information is communicated properly.
- Communicates important information in writing.
- Presents information in a professional manner.
- Presents information effectively at one-to-one and group levels.
- Believes in active listening e.g., summarises checkpoints for understanding and agreed actions.
- Uses a polite and friendly telephone manner.

> "Deep listening is miraculous for both listener and speaker. When someone receives us with openhearted, non-judging, intensely interested listening, our spirits expand."
> – *Sue Patton Thoele*
>
> These [thought] leaders reframe issues, reinterpret the meaning and recreate the passion for achievement. They do all this through the spread and persuasive spell of their thoughts.
> – *Shrinivas Pandit*
> Thought Leaders

Case Studies

From the World of Business

1. Enhancing the Appeal of Titan*

Titan Industries Limited (TIL) began to feel the pressure of stiff competition in 2003. The customer was being offered a wide variety of watches with new designs at affordable prices. It found that it was not safe even at the bottom layer of the pyramid. The grey market, with cheap Chinese imports, and the unorganised sector had cornered a sizeable chunk of the low-end market. The decision to have a suitable brand ambassador for the Titan brand, was thus an attempt to broadbase the appeal of the Titan brand.

In October 2004, with a view to enhancing its universal appeal. Titan Industries Ltd., appointed Aamir Khan as the brand ambassador for its Titan range of watches. Bijou Kurien, Chief Operating Officer (Watches), TIL, said, "There is a perfect fit between Aamir and Titan — their stature, timelessness, and the love and trust they both share with the people, both nationally and internationally, makes this an ideal partnership. Moreover, Aamir has a universal appeal that extends to everyone, across age groups, just as our watches do."

The company wanted its watches to be seen as style and fashion accessories, rather than just utility devices. The company decided to use Aamir in brand and product communication on television and in the print and outdoor media. Aamir Khan was picked after a lot of deliberation. The quality that was finally identified as most critical in Aamir's case was his "universal appeal."

Though the advantages of a vast distribution and service network of TIL had served it well in the 1990s, foreign brands were becoming increasingly popular in the early 2000s, thanks to the change in the retail scenario and the growing affluence of the Indian consumers.

---

* Adapted from ICMR cases/caselets; the original versions can be procured from ICMR/accessed on the ICMR website.

In 2004, besides appointing a brand ambassador, TIL made several attempts to revitalize its sub-brands. It introduced several collections/ranges under each of its sub-brands. Moreover, it participated in the retail boom that the country was experiencing. It opened several outlets in the huge malls and supermarkets that were mushrooming in the big cities. It also paid attention to its communication strategies. Its attempts paid off – the company posted good annual profits and its image was rejuvenated.

Background

TIL, a joint venture between the Tata Group and the Tamil Nadu Industrial Development Corporation, commenced operations in 1987 under the name Titan Watches Limited (TWL). With the diversification of TWL into jewellery in 1994, the company changed its name to TIL. In June 2004, the company diversified into other lifestyle products like eyewear by extending its watch sub-brand Fastrack and perfumery with a new brand *Evolve*, launched in early 2005.

The main manufacturing plants of the company are situated at Hosur in Tamil Nadu. It also has an assembly unit at Dehradun in Uttaranchal and a unit that produced electronic circuitry for quartz watches in Goa. TIL reported a turnover of Rs. 9.58 billion for the year ended 2003-2004.

The Learning

Level-C:
- Identifies communication needs across the organisation and to customers.

Level-B:
- Uses a variety of routes to get the message across.

Other themes covered: Leadership, Planning and Organisation

2. Boundaryless Behaviour – A Lesson from GE*

GE was once a vast organisation of faceless workers with layers of bureaucracy. Jack Welch of GE knew the importance of communication in an organisation and how it could remove impediments in the normal day-to-day activities. At the end of the day this could matter the most. So when he took over as chief, he came up with an idea of "Boundaryless Behaviour".

Jack knew *that would make the difference.* He had a vision of a "boundaryless company" that would remove all the barriers among the various functions of the company: be it engineering, manufacturing, marketing and the rest. For Jack Welch it was both a vision and a strategy.

He stressed on the fact that open-ended communication always fosters growth and development. For the success of an organisation, the thing that matters is how receptive its employees are to the information and how open they are to the ideas from other functions or even other companies.

Open communication is all about bringing new information in to the organisation for its betterment. Jack Welch brought in many new ideas and techniques from other companies. He popularised the line, "Best Practices have legitimised plagiarism," at GE, where the study of other high-performing organisations was institutionalised. Employees were encouraged to borrow and adapt ideas that were not trademarked, patented or proprietary.

Jack Welch visited a Wal-Mart store and observed the speed, the utter customer focus that drove Wal-Mart business. He saw what ideas could be replicated for the benefit of GE.

Soon, 'Boundaryless Behaviour' became the right behaviour at GE. It led to an obsession for finding a better solution, a better idea – be its source a colleague, another GE business or another company on the other side of the globe that would share its practices and ideas with GE.

---

* Adapted from ICMR cases/caselets; the original versions can be procured from ICMR/accessed on the ICMR website.

Jack also instituted a rewards system that recognised the implementer of an idea. By creating this open, sharing climate, he rooted out bureaucracy from the company and developed a workplace where people were open, curious, cooperative and always breaking down barriers.

'Boundaryless Behaviour' completely changed the way people worked, the way they behaved, and it stripped out a whole level of bureaucracy within GE. Boundaryless behaviour increased the organisation's intellectual capital and thus its effectiveness.

The Learning

Level-C:
- Identifies communication needs across the organisation and to customers.

Level-B:
- Identifies and keeps appropriate people at all levels informed (Internal/External)

Level-A:
- Uses the most appropriate communication channel.

Other themes covered: Leadership, Decision making.

3. Bhavarlal Jain – Courageous Communicator*

The Jain Group of Jalgaon, Maharashtra since its establishment in 1963 has committed itself to agriculture. Practically every activity it has undertaken, business or social, is related to this field. At the helm is founder-chairman Bhavarlal Jain (68), who can be credited with putting Jalgaon, a quaint little district town in central Maharashtra, on the world map.

Through his work, Bhavarlal Jain, popularly called *Bhau* (brother), demonstrated that agriculture, the agro-processing

---

* Reproduced with permission, ©McGraw Hill Education, India, B4, Sector 63, Dist. Gautam Budh Nagar, Noida, U.P. 201301.

industry and related business can be made profitable by educating farmers. It is the country's lifeline, in which Bhau saw the opportunity to build a modern agro-business.

In 1963, Jalgaon had no special identity. "I am proud of the fact that we have added value to so many lives and put this quaint little town on the world map."[1] Bhau says with pride, inspiring people by example is the method followed for creating a committed and motivated team. The group received 6 state awards and 57 national awards for outstanding export performance, R&D achievements and entrepreneurship.

Bhau is always ready to explain how Jalgaon came on the world stage: "Micro-irrigation is a scientific method of irrigation, carrying desired water and nutrients directly to the root zone of the plant, drop by drop. Its advantages are early maturity, better quality and higher quantity. It is ideal for problematic soils and water, saves labour and up to 70 per cent water. We are recognised as world leaders in providing custom-made irrigation systems."[2] Jalgaon is the first district town in rural Maharashtra, perhaps in India, to have had a company that raised Rs. 100 crore in a euro issue. This achievement put Jalgaon on the world map.

But then the group met with setbacks as it tried to diversify into new areas. With such a track record of achievements, Bhau did go wrong! It looked strange. But Bhau owned up responsibility and to his error of judgement. His explanation is an example of perfect communication as it resulted in maintaining the trust and goodwill built over years.

On November 26, 1998, Bhavarlal Jain placed a half-page insertion in *The Economic Times*[3] apologizing to his shareholders, suppliers and creditors for his misadventure in diversification. It was probably the first time an Indian corporate leader had chosen this means to make a public apology for bad performance.

---

[1] *Thought Leaders: The Source Code of Exceptional Managers and Entrepreneurs* by Shrinivas Pandit. Tata McGraw-Hill Publishing Company Limited, New Delhi, 2002 (reprint) p.86.
[2] Ibid. p.87
[3] Ibid. p.88

"**I am sad** – that for the first time since our inception, we have fared badly. We ventured into unknown areas like finance, information technology and granite at the cost of our core business... I feel it is my duty to account for, to own up, to admit my misjudgments, to apologise.

I'm happy – that the greatest international recognition in the field of irrigation, the Crawford Reid memorial award, has been bestowed on me. I'm told that only 16 people have won it in the last 19 years and I'm happy that though we burned our fingers venturing into unrelated areas, our employees firmly stood by us, productive as ever. It has been a chastising experience from which we've emerged not unscathed, but financially disciplined, more mature, and certainly more focused.

I'm confident – that despite the hurdles, we can not only bring due recognition to this industry, but also bring about a second green revolution in this country. Because our fundamentals are rock solid. With our voracious appetite for growth and a policy of plowing back profits into our business, I believe there's a lot more we're capable of achieving..."

Such a transparent communication naturally made an impact. It reflected the sincerity of the leader and conveyed the anguish that the man was going through. Bhau's confidence about the future was based on his tested fundamentals on the conduct of business and track record of performance.

The Jain group went through a difficult period, but within three years it was back on track to its original position of strength and trust with its shareholders, distributors and other stakeholders.

> **The Learning**
>
> **Level-C:**
> - Demonstrates originality and flexibility of communication.
>
> **Level-B:**
> - Uses a variety of routes to get the message across.
>
> **Level-A:**
> - Communicates important information in writing.

Other themes covered: Leadership, Personal Responsibility.

4. Hewlett and Packard: The Open-Door Policy*

Stanford engineers, Bill Hewlett and David Packard founded HP in California in 1938 as an electronic instruments company. During the 1940s, HP's products rapidly gained acceptance among engineers and scientists. The company's growth was further aided by heavy purchases by the U.S. government during the Second World War. As their business flourished, the confidence of Hewlett and Packard increased. The founders took pains to explicitly communicate their beliefs and values to the employees through all available means.

Since its inception, HP has been known for its relaxed and open culture. The company follows an "Open-door policy", which encourages employees to discuss their personal and job-related matters with their managers. Most of the employees work in open cubicles while the managers keep their doors open to encourage communication and idea sharing. A typical HP office building has a vast open area, with dozens of cubicles. Most of the employees were technically-oriented engineers who discovered that they actually enjoyed learning and sharing their knowledge. According to Hewlett, "The open-door policy is very important at HP because it characterises the management style to which

---

* Adapted from ICMR cases/caselets; the original versions can be procured from ICMR/accessed on the ICMR website.

we are dedicated. It means managers are available, open and receptive. Every one at HP, including the CEO, work in open plan doorless offices. This ready availability has its drawbacks, in that interruptions are always possible. But at HP, we have found that the benefits of accessibility far outweigh the disadvantages."

The open-door policy became an integral part of the management by objective philosophy. Also, it is a procedure that encourages and, in fact, ensures that communication flow moves both up and down.

The Learning

Level-C:
- Identifies communication needs across the organisation.

Level-B:
- Timely and consistent communication.

Other themes covered: Teamwork.

Interpersonal Skills

2. Influence and Negotiations

*"This meeting for negotiations has been a waste!
We all seem to agree on all the points!"*

Negotiation is a core life-skill. Throughout our lives we are negotiating with someone for something. In fact, a child quickly and instinctively learns some of the basics of negotiation as a matter of survival instinct even before it picks up language.

There are many different definitions of negotiation. We could say that negotiating is "reaching an agreed settlement between two or more parties" or we could define it as "reaching a compromise between conflicting needs". For the purposes of this section, we can define negotiation as, *"The art of getting what you want, even when you don't have direct control over the person who will give it to you"*

With this competency:
One identifies the key motivators of individuals or groups, recognizing underlying objections/concerns; presents own position confidently, using logical argument to persuade others; takes a partnership approach, aiming for a win-win outcome.

LEVELS OF PROFICIENCY

Proficiency Level C

"This is to celebrate our success in negotiations with the union. They have agreed to go slow instead of an outright strike!"

- Influences and convinces others with own enthusiasm and personal style.
- Emphasises risks and benefits to make a persuasive argument for action.
- Backs up argument with facts and data.
- Demonstrates originality and flexibility of communication.
- Identifies communication needs across the organisation and to customers.
- Sees situations as a partnership and aims for a win-win outcome.
- Negotiates lasting agreements among parties with potential conflicting priorities, values and cultural contexts.

> "In business, you don't get what you deserve, you get what you negotiate."
> *– Chester L. Karrass*
>
> "Never cut what you can untie."
> *– Joseph Joubert*
>
> "Start out with an ideal and end up with a deal."
> *– Karl Albrecht*
>
> "If you can't go around it, over it or through it, you had better negotiate with it."
> *– Ashleigh Brilliant*

Influence and Negotiations 33

Proficiency Level B

"Don't talk about information one week old. I have the latest GIS information which says this road is absolutely safe. So let's drive on!"

- Actively seeks out senior management to influence them.
- Anticipates questions and objections, and prepares responses.
- Handles objections skillfully by acknowledging issues and putting forward alternatives.
- Involves all relevant people to gain their agreement.
- Identifies factors which are of particular interest to others.
- Sells the wider benefits of their preferred approach

"Negotiation in the classic diplomatic sense assumes parties more anxious to agree than to disagree."
– *Dean Acheson*

"It's just as unpleasant to get more than you bargain for as to get less."
– *George Bernard Shaw*

Proficiency Level A

"It is a step forward. Now we have agreed to meet more often to resolve the issues!"

- Uses the most appropriate communication channel e.g., e-mail, telephone, face to face.
- Presents own position using persuasive style and language.
- Stresses the benefits of the approach being proposed.
- Gains buy-in by getting others to see advantages.
- Negotiates, internally and externally.
- Willing to compromise to achieve outcomes and overcome obstacles.
- Seeks closure.
- Uses third parties to resolve conflicts, when appropriate.

> "Given a fair wind, we will negotiate our way into the Common Market, head held high, not crawling in. Negotiations? Yes. Unconditional acceptance of whatever terms are offered us? No."
> – *Harold Wilson*
>
> "He who makes a timid request invites denial."
> – *Seneca*

Case Studies

From the World of Business

1. Averting Strike at Bangalore

This happened in the late seventies and it brings out the qualities that a conciliator or mediator must have, to intervene in an industrial dispute. Conciliation is a part of the government's industrial relations system to ensure that an industrial dispute has a good chance of settlement and does not precipitate into a strike or lockout. In those days Bangalore-based Public Sector Undertakings, employed nearly 80,000 workers and had their major facilities and corporate offices located at Bangalore. There was Hindustan Aeronautics Limited (HAL), Bharat Earth Movers Limited (BEML), Bharat Electronics Limited (BEL), Indian Telephone Industries (ITI), and Hindustan Machine Tools (HMT). A strike would not only have caused immense financial loss but perhaps triggered a law and order problem in the city.

A strike in these industries was imminent after the failure of bipartite negotiations over a dispute on wages and allowances. This was averted by marathon conciliation proceedings initiated by the State Labour Commissioner, which ended in a settlement in the early hours of the morning when the strike was to commence. At the last minute practically, the compromise formula offered by the Labour Commissioner was accepted. It was a complex situation as there were many stakeholders apart from the immediate management and workers, including the state and central government and parent ministries. The negotiations succeeded because the effort satisfied what Prof G. Richard Shell spells out as the three most critical inputs: proper alignment of interests, effective handling of bargaining process, and respect for basic human sensitivities or psychology.

A review of the conciliation proceedings shows interesting features. The informal team of conciliators consisted of Labour Commissioner, Additional Labour Commissioner, and Deputy Labour Commissioner (Industrial Relations) and though only three of the five public sector undertakings were declared as

Public Utility Services, where conciliation was mandatory, conciliation proceedings were held for all the five Central Public Sector Undertakings.

Separate and joint meetings of the committees, representing the management and the unions were held. Informal discussions were held from time to time with trade union leaders and management representatives, on the days on which conciliation proceedings were not fixed, following an 'open-door policy'. A direct appeal was made to the trade union leaders to defer the strike and keep the dialogue going by following 'forget the clock policy'. The State government was kept informed from time to time about the progress of negotiations. The conciliator kept in mind that conciliation was only an assisted-bargaining process and an extension of collective bargaining. So the parties were given full freedom to negotiate themselves. After a few attempts, hard-liners and soft-liners were identified, and efforts were made to build up a consensus through soft-liners on both sides. This strategy paid off. On the last day, the talks continued deep into the night and the exhausted negotiators were more than relieved when a settlement was reached.

The chief conciliator took care to avoid the five A's, which P. D. Shenoy in his book describes as Anger, Arrogance, Argument, Annoyance, and Anxiety. At the same time success was achieved because he displayed an amiable nature along with Honesty, Helpfulness, Patience, and Stamina.

The Learning

Level-C:
- Identifies the key motivators of individuals or groups, and identifies underlying objections/concerns.

Level-B:
- Involves all relevant people to gain their agreement.

Level-A:
- Willing to compromise to achieve outcomes and overcome obstacles.

Other themes covered: Communication, Decision making

2. E. Sreedharan: Iconic Project Manager

E. Sreedharan, an engineer who started his career with the railways, though not a conventional business leader, has become a living legend for demonstrating top managerial qualities and result-oriented corporate culture in the realm of mega public sector projects. No other manager has achieved so much in terms of creating public infrastructure in so short a time within the government system. Reputed for beating deadlines and keeping within financial outlays ever since he repaired a damaged Pamban bridge in Tamil Nadu in a record 45 days, he took on the two mega projects that made him an iconic manager after retirement - the Konkan rail project and the Delhi Metro. In 2005, after completion of the first phase of the metro, he wanted to finally retire but the government persuaded him to continue for another three-year term as the chief of the DMRC. Though in his mid seventies, Sreedharan has many lessons for younger people; he has excelled as a team leader and achiever due to a number of competencies, including his ability to influence people, negotiate terms that would enable him to function at his best, and lead by example.

Executing a project of such a mammoth proportion as Delhi Metro, had its share of challenges. A team had to be chosen, contracts had to be signed and tenders placed, deadlines had to be set and met, traffic needed to be regulated, and finances managed. All this had to be done without causing an iota of inconvenience to the Delhiite behind the wheels. "We had an able and experienced team leader in Sreedharan. He spelt out the mission statement and the corporate culture clearly to one and all," says the chief public relations officer of DMRC, Anuj Dayal. Sreedharan's personality and reputation was a critical factor. He instilled strong team spirit and dedication to work in the team members, as he led by example.

The leader defined 'corporate culture' as: integrity of executives and staff should be beyond doubt; punctuality is the key word; targets are most sacrosanct; organisation must be lean but effective; corporation must project an image of efficiency, transparency, courtesy, and 'we-mean-business' attitude; and construction should not lead to environmental degradation. What contributed, in no small measure, to DMRC's success was the autonomy given to the managing director. Sreedharan took up this task on the condition that he should be allowed to choose his own team and enjoyed a fair degree of autonomy.

Though a lot of technology has come from abroad, DMRC has a clause inserted into the contract with companies that they must have an Indian partner. Consequently, the DMRC is procuring the trains from Bharat Earth Movers Limited, Bangalore and elevators are also being produced indigenously. Another feature is the punctuality with which the DMRC pays its contractors or 'associates' along with strict monitoring of targets.

In the past six years, the DMRC has also re-defined public relations to a large extent. In ensuring minimum inconvenience to motorists and pedestrians alike, the DMRC successfully converted a challenge into an opportunity. All utilities were diverted in advance to ensure that there was no disruption of water, electricity, sewerage, and telephone connections during the construction of the area. Barricades were put up. An alternate traffic plan was drawn up with the help of the Indian Institute of Technology, Delhi and in collaboration with Delhi Police. Also, new roads were built or the existing roads widened to accommodate traffic. The DMRC organised community interaction programmes for re-dressing problems that arose among the local people.

Every Monday, heads of each department would meet and set new or review targets. A kind of reverse clock displays remaining days before the target date for specific works. It is obvious Sreedharan's ability to influence people and negotiate his terms comes from his commitment to work and self-less leadership.

The Learning

Level-C:
- Influences and convinces others with own enthusiasm and personal style.
- Sees situations as a partnership and aims for a win-win outcome.

Level-B:
- Sells the wider benefits of their preferred approach.

Other themes covered: Decision making, Leadership

3. Philips India: To Sell or Not?

A top management business decision can often trigger conflict with workers. This case discusses the conflict between Philips India and its workers after Philips India Limited (PIL) announced its decision to sell the colour television factory to Kitchen Appliances Limited, a subsidiary of Videocon.

By mid 1996, PIL's capacity-expansion plans had fallen way behind the set targets. The workers also started raising voices against the management and asked for a hike in wages as well. PIL claimed that the workers were already overpaid and underproductive. The employees held that they continued to work inspite of the irregular hike in wages. These differences resulted in a 20-month long confrontation over the wage hike issue; the go-slow tactics of the workers and the declining production, resulted in huge losses for the company.

In May 1998, PIL announced its decision to stop operations at Salt Lake and production was halted in June 1998. In December 1998, a resolution was passed at PIL's annual general meeting (AGM) with a 51 per cent vote in favour of the sale.

The workers were surprised and angry at the decision. Philips Employee Union (PEU) president found the management's decision a major *volte-face* considering its efforts at promoting it and then adding capacity every year. Others said that the sale would not profit the company in any way. The Salt Lake factory was state-of-the-art with enough capacity. Being close to Kolkata port, shipping of components from Far Eastern countries was much easier. Also, PIL's major market was in the eastern region.

Over Rs. 70 crore had been invested in the plant. The union challenged PIL's plan of selling the CTV unit at such a low price of Rs 9 crore as against a valuation of Rs 30 crore made by Dalal Consultants as independent valuers. However, the management contended that a voluntary retirement scheme (VRS) offer at the CTV unit would cost the company Rs 21 crore. Refuting this, senior members of the union said, "There is no way that a VRS at the CTV unit can set Philips back by more than Rs 9.2 crore." The unions even approached the Dhoots of Videocon with an offer of Rs 10 crore in an attempt to outbid Videocon. They claimed that they could pay the amount from their provident fund, cooperative savings and personal savings. But PIL rejected the offer claiming that it was legally bound to sell to Videocon. But if the offer fell through, then the union's offer would be considered.

The workers did not trust Videocon to be a good employer and were afraid that it might not be able to pay their wages. Evidence was produced of Videocon's failure to make payments in time during the course of its transactions with Philips.

In March 1999, the Kolkata High Court passed an order restraining any further deal on the sale of the factory. The reason given was that the transfer price was too low and PIL needed to view it from a more practical perspective.

But PIL refused to accept defeat. The company immediately revealed its plans to take further legal action and complete the sale at any cost. The company said that the matter was beyond the trial court's jurisdiction and its interference was unwarranted, as the price had been a negotiated one. So PIL moved the Supreme Court.

In December 2000, the Supreme Court finally passed judgment on the controversial Philips case. It was in favour of PIL. The judge said that though the workers could demand for their rights, they had no say in any of the policy decisions of the company, if their interests were not adversely affected.

The top management decision was thus pursued to its logical conclusion.

The Learning

Level-C:
- Backs up argument with facts and data.

Level-B:
- Handles objections skillfully by acknowledging issues and putting forward alternatives.

Other themes covered: Decision making.

Interpersonal Skills

3. Building Relationships

"He is not able to keep step with his boss... there is tension between them!"

For the success of the organisation as a whole, it is very important that a leader maintains good relationships across all the levels in the organisation. Why is it so important? First, this helps the organisation to get more out of its employees, as people go the extra mile for those they trust and respect. Second, being on good terms with your team helps ensure a flow of accurate information through both formal and informal channels. Finally, maintaining good relationships makes dissatisfaction less likely and enables one to nip potential problems in the bud.

With this competency:

One is sensitive to the needs of others, demonstrating interest in their views; takes a supportive approach, showing empathy to others' situation; builds relationships across all levels, business groups and locations; and demonstrates sensitivity to other cultures, exhibiting tact and diplomacy.

Levels of Proficiency

Proficiency Level C

"This meeting has been specially called to reach a quick consensus on critical issues!"

- Manages a wide network of professional relationships, inside and outside the organisation and uses them effectively to develop business.
- Activates formal and informal channels to develop new contacts and more effective internal and external relationships.
- Manages conflicts, facilitating open discussion.
- Develops relationships with opinion leaders and/or high-level experts.
- Identifies potential barriers to cooperation among groups.
- Actively builds personal networks e.g., across business groups/locations, externally.

> "People are lonely because they build walls instead of bridges."
> – *Joseph F. Newton*

> "Each friend represents a world in us, a world possibly not born until they arrive, and it is only by this meeting that a new world is born."
> – *Anais Nin*

> "The bond that links your true family is not one of blood, but of respect and joy in each other's life. Rarely do members of one family grow up under the same roof."
> – *Richard Bach*

Building Relationships

Proficiency Level B

"He belongs to a different culture. Perhaps that is the victory sign in his country!"

- Takes a supportive approach, not blaming others for mistakes.
- Seeks to understand others underlying motivation.
- Builds trust by being open and honest in dealings with others.
- Takes impact on employees into account when dealing with problems.
- Sensitive to the needs and expectations of other cultures.
- Recognises nuances of behaviour in cross-cultural relationships.

"Every person, all the events of your life are there because you have drawn them there. What you choose to do with them is up to you."
– *Richard Bach*

"I've learned in my lifetime so far that you can't help who you fall for and no matter how hard you try and how much it hurts you everyday, that you just wanna be with them or just talk to them, you never stop trying to make them happy by the little things you say or do because that's what makes your life worth going on for."
– *Unknown*

Proficiency Level A

"Tell your staff I dress, think and talk like a man!"

- Builds relationships at all levels.
- Consults with others to gain their views.
- Gives and receives feedback constructively.
- Shows consideration for others' situations, needs, feelings and views.
- Balances different parties' expectations.
- Thinks about future impact of own behaviour

> "The most acute social priority is for individuals to clean up their own mental and emotional messes."
> – *Doc Childre*
>
> "Nothing splendid has ever been achieved except by those who dared believe that something inside them was superior to circumstance."
> – *Bruce Barton*

Case Studies

From the World of Business

1. Biocon Leader – Kiran Mazumdar*

Kiran Mazumdar-Shaw is the founder-chairperson of the Biocon Group, which is India's largest producer and exporter of novel industrial enzymes. In November 2004, she received the 'Business Woman of the year Award' from the *Economic Times of India* symbolizing the increasing importance of the role of women in Indian business. Kiran has some special skills worth studying.

Kiran is a very people-oriented person. She has always practiced a people-friendly approach in Biocon and succeeded in keeping petty politics and insecurities at minimum.

She encouraged people to address her as 'Kiran' throughout the organisation, right from the workshop operator to her senior colleagues. This created a bond all around. She encouraged her people to wander to various divisions and interact with anyone and every one. She kept herself abreast of everything in all departments by paying them unscheduled visits (reminiscent of GE under Jack Welch). She employed young, bright people and energised them with zeal to excel. She ended up being a good team builder.

At Biocon, from the start, there was no formal bar to approach anyone directly and this holds true across the company. This free crossflow of interactions has made the company very interactive and innovative.

Effective bonding, thus, takes place between people in organisations without boundaries. Structural flexibility allows people free interaction and status barriers are minimised. Employees in Biocon are more satisfied with their jobs as they can approach anybody with their problem without any hesitation. Kiran learned a lot from her mother especially about managing people. The right job for the right person is a winning formula. "Underlying all this is my ethos that it is people who make an organisation, and that HRD is the most

---

* Reproduced with permission, ©McGraw Hill Education, India, B4, Sector 63, Dist. Gautam Budh Nagar, Noida, U.P. 201301.

important function of all CEOs. I do believe we have excellent people in our organisation, and *we have found an effective way in which we get ordinary people to do extraordinary things, and to do ordinary things extraordinarily well.*"[1]

Kiran feels that apart from the benefits of technical collaboration with Biocon Ireland that started in 1978, she has gained a lot from Les Auchincloss, the founder of Biocon. He gave her insights needed to create a boundaryless organisation. He also ingrained in her the belief in promoting personal rapport with her key people and building a good team of like-minded professionals.

The Learning

Level-C:
- Actively builds personal networks e.g., across business groups/locations externally.

Level-B:
- Builds trust by being open and honest in dealing with others.

Level-A:
- Builds relationships at all levels.

Other themes covered: Communication, Leadership, Influence and Negotiation.

2. HR Visionary – Narayana Murthy*

Infosys Technologies Ltd., the globally-recognised Indian software major, as is well-known, amazed every one with a dazzling performance in just over two decades after it was established. Its founder-chairman and chief mentor Narayana Murthy, is a committed wealth creator and leader who has always lived the principles he has preached. He has deservedly reached iconic status for millions of admirers.

---

[1] *Thought Leaders: The Source Code of Exceptional Managers and Entrepreneurs* by Shrinivas Pandit. Tata McGraw-Hill Publishing Company Limited, New Delhi, 2002 (reprint) p.204.

* Reproduced with permission, ©McGraw Hill Education, India, B4, Sector 63, Dist. Gautam Budh Nagar, Noida, U.P. 201301.

Murthy had a vision in his mind, which helped him make Infosys into a company respected across the globe. The success of Infosys can be attributed to the human and technical skills of Murthy that he successfully applied to real business situations.

Murthy was quick to realize that he was going to depend on human resource. He knew that software is a knowledge business and knowledge resides in human beings. Therefore, he valued the importance of interpersonal relationships and shifted his focus to brainware from software. Says Murthy, "Since we want to attract and retain high-quality professionals, we protect and enhance the respect for professionals."[1] Experts feel that one factor which helped Infosys to grow at a faster pace than others was the low employee turnover. The turnover rate at Infosys was around 11 per cent as opposed to industry average of over 25 per cent during the 1990s. Infosys retention capability was an end result of its proactive HR practices.

Murthy was sensitive to the needs of his employees. Infosys provided world-class facilities to them: a quality day-care centre, trained teachers, an exercise centre, tennis and golf, fully staffed medicare center, highly-subsidised cafeteria, indoor games, buses to ferry to and from office, crèche facilities for kids, credit cards or house loan applications and flexible working hours. Infosys was one of the first companies to adopt an employee stock option plan (ESOP) and create additional wealth for its employees. Murthy believed that employees created wealth and unless Infosys had a mechanism to make them principal shareholders, it was unlikely to grow. By 1997, 500 employees were awarded stock under the ESOP. By 2001, Infosys had about 2000 rupee millionaires on its staff and more than 213-dollar millionaires. On the other side, Murthy was equally sensitive to the importance of keeping customers and investors happy. Building long-term relations on the basis of trust was critical. Two things he always emphasised:

---

[1] *Thought Leaders: The Source Code of Exceptional Managers and Entrepreneurs* by Shrinivas Pandit. Tata McGraw-Hill Publishing Company Limited, New Delhi, 2002 (reprint) p.241

"Growth comes from repeat business which comes from relationships" and "Investors want us to operate as trustees."[2]

All these measures taken to manage people did pay off. *Asiamoney* published from Hong Kong, declared Infosys as the best managed company. This was just one of the many accolades that the company received.

The Learning

Level-C:
- Manages a wide network of professional relationships, inside and outside the organisation and uses them effectively to develop business.

Level-B:
- Builds trust by being open and honest in dealings with others.

Level-A:
- Builds relationships at all levels.

Other themes covered: Leadership, Planning and Organisation, Business focus.

3. B. M. Munjal: The Hero Group

B. M. Munjal (Brij Mohanlall Munjal) is the Chairman of the Hero Group. He is a first generation entrepreneur who started very small and through sheer hard work and perseverance made it to the top. Today, Hero Group is the largest manufacturer of two-wheelers in the world and B. M. Munjal is the man widely credited with its success.

B. M. Munjal's journey began in 1944 at the age of 20. Brij Mohanlall along with his three brothers, Dayanand (32), Satyanand (27) and Om Prakash (16) moved from their birthplace, Kamalia in Pakistan to Amritsar. The brothers started supplying components to the local bicycle business. After partition in 1947, the family was forced to move to Ludhiana. The town was already a major hub of the Indian

---

[2] Ibid. p. 241

bicycle business and an important textile center. The Munjals slowly spread their bicycle component distribution network in other parts of the country and became one of India's largest bicycle parts suppliers. In 1952, Munjals made a shift from supplying to manufacturing, starting initially with cycle handlebars, front forks and chains.

In 1956, the Punjab state government announced the issue of twelve new industrial licenses to make bicycles in Ludhiana. The Munjal brothers seized this opportunity. Helped by the Punjab government's financial support to supplement their own limited capital resources, the Munjals set up Hero Cycles. Hero Cycles was registered as a 'large-scale industrial unit' and it initially produced 7,500 units per year.

Soon Hero Cycles started giving well-established players such as Raleigh, Hind Cycles and Atlas Cycles stiff competition. The hero cycle was comparatively cheaper and was sturdy and reliable. It gave the customers value for their money.

In January 1984, Japan's Honda, the world's largest manufacturer of motorcycles, elicited interest in collaborating with the Hero Group to manufacture motorcycles in India. An agreement was signed, and on 13 April 1985 the first Hero Honda motor bike was rolled out. Today, the company is the largest manufacturer of motorcycles in the world.

For his outstanding contribution to the success of Hero Group, B. M. Munjal was honoured with Ernst & Young's, 'Entrepreneur of the Year' award in 2001.

Today, the Hero Group comprises of 20 companies, 300 ancillary suppliers, a deep market penetration with over 5,000 outlets, 23,000 plus employees and has a turnover of U.S.$ 3.20 billion (FY 2006).

The growth of the Group through the years has been influenced by a number of factors.

The Hero Group through the Hero Cycles Division was the first to introduce the concept of just-in-time inventory. The Group boasts of superb operational efficiencies. Every assembly line worker operates two machines simultaneously to save time and improve productivity. An interesting fact is that most of the machines are either developed or fabricated in-house, which has resulted in low inventory levels.

In Hero Cycles Limited, the just-in-time inventory principle has been working since the beginning of production in the unit and is functional even till date. The raw material vendors bring in the goods, get paid instantly and by the end of the day the finished product is rolled out of the factory. This is the Japanese style of production and in India, Hero is probably the first company to have mastered the art of the just-in-time inventory principle.

Ancillarisation:
An integral part of the group strategy of doing business differently was providing support to ancillary units. This has created stable long-term relations. There are over 300 ancillary units today whose production is dedicated to Hero's requirements and also a large number of other vendors, which include some of the better-known companies in the automotive segment.

The Munjals have gone much beyond the conventional definition of ancillarisation, making it a point to extend technical and managerial support to these ancillaries. These ancillary units are manned by friends, relatives, ex-employees or close associates of the Munjal family, since the Group patriarch, Brij Mohanlall would say he "... never wanted to march alone."

Employee policy:
Another striking feature within the Hero Group is the commitment and dedication of its workers. There is no organised labour union and family members of employees find ready employment within Hero. The philosophy with regard to labour management is – "Hero is growing, grow with Hero."

When it comes to workers' benefits, the Hero Group is known for providing facilities quite ahead of the industry norms. Long before other companies did so, Hero was giving its employees a uniform allowance, as well as House Rent Allowance (HRA) and Leave Travel Allowance (LTA). Extra benefits took the form of medical check-ups, not just for workers but also for the immediate family members.

Dealer Network:

The relationship of the Munjals with their dealers is unique in its closeness. The dealers are considered a part of the Hero family. With a nationwide dealer network comprising of over 5,000 outlets, the Munjals have a formidable distribution system in place.

Sales agents from Hero travel to all the corners of the country, visiting dealers and send back daily postcards with information on the stock position of that day, turnover, fresh purchases, anticipated demand and also competitor action in the region. The manufacturing units have a separate department to handle dealer complaints and problems, and the first response is always given within 24 hours.

Financial Planning:

The Hero Group benefits from the Group Chairman's financial acumen and his grasp of technology, manufacturing and marketing. Group Company, Hero Cycles Limited has one of the highest labour productivity rates in the world. In Hero Honda Motors Limited, the focus is on financial and raw material management and a low-employee turnover.

Consolidated Family Business:

The Hero Group is a strong family run business. There is no other Group that has so successfully managed to stay together for nearly 50 years. The system is to bring in any new family member, coming of age, within the fold of the existing business or set him up in a new business. The third generation is already actively involved in the existing as well as the new initiatives within the Group. The Group's future is being consolidated with the same zeal by the second and the third generations of the family, aided by workers who typify the hardy spirit of the Punjab.

Diversification:

Throughout the years of mammoth growth, the Group Chairman, Brij Mohanlall has actively looked at diversification. A significant level of backward integration in its manufacturing activities has been a substantial factor in the Group's growth and has led to the establishment of the

Hero Cycles Cold Rolling Division, Munjal and Sunbeam Castings, Munjal Auto Components and Munjal Showa Limited amongst other component-manufacturing units.

Then there was the expansion into the automotive segment with the setting up of Majestic Auto Limited, where the first indigenously designed moped, Hero Majestic, went into commercial production in 1978. Then came Hero Motors which introduced Hero Puch, in collaboration with global technology leader Steyr Daimler Puch of Austria. Hero Honda Motors was established in 1984 to manufacture 1000 cc motorcycles.

The Munjals have more recently moved into other segments like exports, financial services and information technology, which includes customer response services and software development. Further expansion is expected in the areas of insurance and telecommunication.

The Hero Group's phenomenal growth is the result of constant innovations and dynamic leadership of the Group Chairman, characterised by an ethos of entrepreneurship and building stronger relationships with investors, partners, vendors, dealers and customers.

The Learning

Level-C:
- Manages a wide network of professional relationships, inside and outside the organisation and uses them effectively to develop business.

Level-B:
- Builds trust by being open and honest in dealings with others.

Level-A:
- Builds relationships at all levels.

Other themes covered: Leadership, Business focus, Planning and Organisation

People Development

1. Teamwork

"Now how am I ever going to make a team out of them?"

Working together as a team means no one person but everyone together is responsible for the success of the team. Good teams share some basic elements to be a high energy team. Whether you are forming a new team or helping to rejuvenate an established team, you need team spirit and patience. There is no such thing as a quick team fix. Margerison and McCann (1985) spent many years working with teams. Through their research they have found that many teams fail because they do not understand what their purpose is and have no clear picture of where they are heading.

With this competency:

One works cooperatively with others towards a shared, common goal; makes best use of different knowledge skills and personal styles within the team; and is willing to put team objectives above personal goals.

LEVELS OF PROFICIENCY

Proficiency Level C

"All three of you must return for camp by sun down. I have split the equipment in three packs so even if one of you fails to turn up, we all have a problem!"

- Identifies the area where individual performance could improve by way of sharing of efforts and ideas.
- Provides assistance and advice on the various aspects connected to the roles in the group.
- Effectively manages dissent as a moment of confrontation and integration.
- Recognises and makes the most of the other group member's contribution, promoting cohesion and performance development.
- Creates empowerment, giving responsibility for common objectives to group members, manages conflicts by maintaining a positive environment.

"Individually, we are one drop. Together, we are an ocean."
– *Ryunosuke Satoro*

"Teamwork is the ability to work together toward a common vision; the ability to direct individual accomplishments toward organisational objectives. It is the fuel that allows common people to attain uncommon results."
– *Unknown*

"Individual commitment to a group effort – that is what makes a team work, a company work, a society work, a civilisation work."
– *Vince Lombardi*

Proficiency Level B

"Hello! Get off the line you ass! Sorry sir, not you ! I am Johnson the chief coordinator. Hello, what about the next delivery? What do you mean what delivery?

- Creates a sense of team spirit within and across the business.
- Coordinates teams across the organisation and country boundaries.
- Creates awareness of (and makes best use of) different styles within the team.

> "The nice thing about teamwork is that you always have others on your side."
> – *Margaret Carty*
>
> "If everyone is moving forward together, then success takes care of itself."
> – *Henry Ford*
>
> "When a team outgrows individual performance and learns team confidence, excellence becomes a reality."
> – *Joe Paterno*

Proficiency Level A

"Hello! Can I help? You chaps don't look very happy! And I am ready to diffuse the conflict!"

- Provides personal support to other team members in times of trouble.
- Shares and gains knowledge and learning from others to resolve problems.
- Discusses problems with colleagues.
- Involves others to assist and resolve issues.
- Shows appreciation to other team members for assistance.
- Gives time to ensure others understand; is approachable
- Cooperates with others to ensure objectives are achieved.

> The leaders who work most effectively, it seems to me, never say 'I'. And that's not because they have trained themselves not to say 'I'. They don't think 'I.' They think 'we'; they think 'team'. They understand their job to be to make the team function. They accept responsibility and don't sidestep it, but 'we' gets the credit... This is what creates trust, what enables you to get the task done.
> – *Peter Drucker*
>
> "One man can be a crucial ingredient on a team, but one man cannot make a team."
> – *Kareem Abdul-Jabbar*

Case Studies

From the World of Business

1. The Dabbawalas of Mumbai

The dabbawalas of Mumbai are acknowledged as one of the best cases of network management in the world. The dabbawalas date back to the late 19th century and more than 120 years later these tiffin carriers are still functioning in an uniquely effective manner.

How do the tiffin boxes magically reach their correct destination? For this purpose, each tiffin box is colour coded and marked with sign/s, such as MD for Marine Drive – according to its final destination.

Each box also carries a code to ensure it returns to its correct place of origin. The entire system depends on teamwork and meticulous timing. The tiffins are collected from homes between 7.00 a.m. and 9:00 a.m. and taken to the nearest railway station. At various intermediary stations, they are brought down on to the platforms and sorted out for areawise distribution. For example, at Ville Parle Station there are four groups of dabbawallas and each group has 20 members and each member serves 40 customers. That makes 3,200 tiffins in all. These 3200 tiffins are collected by 9.00 a.m., reach the station and are sorted out according to their destinations. Next the 80 dabbawallas re-group according to the numbers of tiffins to be delivered in Grant Road Station area, then 4 people are assigned to that station, keeping in mind that each area person can carry no more than 35-40 tiffins. During the earlier sorting process each dabbawala would have concentrated on locating only those 40 tiffins under his charge and this specialisation makes the entire system almost totally error free. Depending on the distance a tiffin has to commute, it takes a train, a cycle or a cart ride or is carried on the shoulder of the dabbawala.

The majority of the dabbawalas come from the neighbouring towns and villages of western Maharashtra. They are bound by a strong social bond and a common language. More recently they have organised into an association called Mumbai Tiffin Box Suppliers Association, which operates on a simple management structure.

It is very significant that the *Forbes Magazine* recently awarded the dabbawalas a Six Sigma performance rating which has put them in the same rank as GE and Motorola as far as efficiency and quality of service are concerned. Six Sigma rating means that it is almost totally an error free system. Daily about 2,00,000 meals are delivered by the system at an average cost of Rs. 325 per month. Among the great fans of this network we have Prince Charles of England and Richard Branson and both have come and met these unique people. The dabba operation has been the subject of field study of many a business school and even of documentaries from India and abroad.

Most of these dabbawallas are illiterate or have dropped out of school, but they are the ultimate practitioners of logistics management. The 4500 tiffin carriers meet and exchange tiffin boxes at public places like the railway station, and without causing a jam or confusion, lunch boxes are sorted out and exchanged quickly with absolutely zero involvement of documentation.

The system works so effectively due to three factors – plenty of commuters, an efficient and widespread railway network and large distances between the workplaces and the places of residence. And ultimately due to the dabbawallas who are the ultimate practitioners of logistics management and teamwork.

The Learning

Level-C:
- Identifies the area where individual performance could improve by way of sharing of efforts and ideas.

Level-B:
- Creates sense of team spirit within and across business.

Level-A:
- Cooperates with others to ensure objectives are achieved.

Other themes covered: Planning and Organisation, Service Focus

2. K. M. Birla: Visionary Team Builder

K. M. Birla is proud of his heritage and legacy. He credits his elders with giving him certain values and also encouraging him to take his own business decisions. No wonder he has managed to create a brand by himself and has become one of India's most respected businessmen.

Kumar's greatest challenge has been to promote a distinct management style quite different from the old school of his father Aditya Birla or even G. D. Birla. Comparing his style with his father's, who was more hands-on, Kumar says: "My style is to give people much more freedom to do their own thing. As long as they deliver, I don't need to get involved... I am available if they need me and I will hold them accountable, but I will not interfere needlessly."[1] While Aditya Birla was great in one-to-one motivation and contact, Kumar is more group oriented and likes to motivate groups of people. He feels that in business, "it is more important to empower a whole group of people than to depend on a single individual..." Kumar has indeed succeeded by empowering teams and promoting merit.[2]

Birla's faith in meritocracy is seen in his decisions. In his father's time, there were several marwaris in the top management. Today there are plenty of non-marwaris and there is a sense that merit would be recognised by the company.

Birla wants strict adherence to policies that have been discussed and approved even when it is not an easy choice. For example, he introduced a retirement policy, similar to the one Ratan Tata introduced at the Tata Group. Birla's retirement policy saw over three hundred senior executives, between 62 and 65 years, step down after years of service. Though the policy was drafted in 2001, he took a year to implement, giving the target staff enough time to plan their retirement life. He then hired 190 young executives to infuse fresh and out-of-the-box thinking in the group. "I think its been one of the most important decisions I've had to make," says Birla. He places a lot of emphasis on HR and hired a top HR expert to spearhead the group's HR initiatives.

---

[1] *Men of Steel* by Vir Sanghvi, Roli Books, New Delhi 2007. p. 18
[2] Ibid.

People skills are Birla's biggest strength. He has the ability to get on with both the older guard and the new generation. Soft spoken but persuasive, Birla likes to be directly involved and he sends individual notes to employees regarding their performance or when he feels necessary.

The Learning

Level-C:
- Creates empowerment, giving responsibility for common objectives to group members; manages conflicts, maintaining a positive environment.

Level-B:
- Coordinates teams across the organisation and country boundaries.

Other themes covered: Leadership, Building Capability

3. Infosys – Building Teams on Core Values*

Infosys grew from a small one-room office to an IT giant which has received worldwide acclaim for more than one reason. What is the root cause? Murthy, the legendary founder of Infosys has been out-and-out a systems thinker. Murthy's strength has always been his ability to connect emotionally, his strong faith in middle class value system, and the way he puts human resource on top of every other input in business. He has always managed to put the right person on the right job. He has shown an uncanny ability to put together a mutually exclusive but collectively exhaustive set of skills, whether for a venture or a project. The rise of Infosys is in fact, the story of his expertise in creating an enabling environment, building customer relationship on trust, spotting business opportunities and perhaps most of all, creating and then sharing wealth.

Murthy leveraged these strengths in putting systems in place in the husbanding of HR, from selection to retention,

---

* Reproduced with permission, ©McGraw Hill Education, India, B4, Sector 63, Dist. Gautam Budh Nagar, Noida, U.P. 201301.

to the novel Employee Stock Option Plan (ESOP). He brought in globally-accepted best practices in corporate governance and adopting a global delivery system which increased predictability in deliverables. Murthy is indeed a proud man whenever he talks of the principles that Infosys has demonstrated, particularly for the young IT generation. These are briefly as follows:

- It is possible for professionals to stay back in India and create wealth.
- It is possible to conduct business honestly.
- Sharing wealth with employees only increases your own wealth.
- Investors reward you if you adhere to the best principles of corporate governance and level with them at all points of time.
- It is possible to benchmark against global standards in India.
- Putting the public good ahead of the private good would result in enriching the private good.

He is also justifiably proud of his *ability to assess people*. He says, "I am most proud of putting a team together, inculcating values, creating an environment of absolute professionalism and being able to assess the person as well as the professional." The typical Infosys professional, according to Murthy has to be open minded, able to learn to work with other people and "willing to forget old things and ask at all times the questions: How am I bringing value to the table? How far can I take an idea that has a market? How can I put together a team and add value? No specific degree is required."[1]

Murthy feels that for creating an enabling environment *the most vital input is human emotion*. He says, "Unless you demonstrate your emotions you cannot get commitment, because people want to relate emotionally. You have to give positive strokes, then only can you give negative feedback."[2]

---

[1] *Thought Leaders* . . . op. cit. p.238
[2] Ibid. p.239

The Learning

Level-C:
- Recognises and makes the most of the other group member's contribution, promoting cohesion and performance development.

Level-B:
- Creates awareness of (and makes best use of) different styles within the team.

Level-A:
- Shares and gains knowledge and learning from others to resolve problems.
- Cooperates with others to ensure objectives are achieved.

Other themes covered: Leadership, Building Capability

People Development

2. Leadership

"I have brought you this far. Now one of you take the lead up to the final goal!"

Leadership is a process by which a person influences others to accomplish an objective and directs the organisation in a way that makes it more cohesive and coherent. Leaders carry out this process by applying their leadership attributes, such as beliefs, values, ethics, character, knowledge and communication skills.

Though many would not agree, good leaders are *made* not born. Good leaders develop through a never-ending process of self-study, education, training and experience. To inspire workers into higher levels of teamwork, there are certain things one must *do, know, and, be*. These qualities are acquired through continual work and study.

With this competency:

One creates a vision, sets high standards and convinces others to strive towards them; clarifies objectives and responsibilities for individuals and teams; motivates others and empowers them by showing trust in them and their ability to deliver results; takes personal accountability for activity and results within own area of responsibility.

LEVELS OF PROFICIENCY
Proficiency Level C

"That resort on the top of the hill touching the skies... a symbol of ultimate glory for our company!"

- Promotes organisational processes that support the vision.
- Implements systems and processes that promote personal responsibility.
- Creates an environment that promotes ownership and accountability at all levels.

> "Management is doing things right; leadership is doing the right things."
> *– Peter F. Drucker*
>
> "Most companies don't die because they are wrong; most die because they don't commit themselves... You have to have a strong leader setting a direction. And it doesn't even have to be the best direction – just a strong, clear one."
> *– Andy Grove*

Proficiency Level B

"Sir, you will need this stool to show the peaking of our profits!"

- Creates a clear vision and direction for the business.
- Sets high standards.
- Takes accountability for self and team.
- Defines roles clearly.
- Champions the team's interests within the business.
- Empowers team – allows them to make decisions within their area.

> "The very essence of leadership is that you have to have a vision. You can't blow an uncertain trumpet."
> – *Theodore Hesburgh*

> "The best executive is the one who has sense enough to pick good men to do what he wants done, and self-restraint to keep from meddling with them while they do it."
> – *Theodore Roosevelt*

> "Don't tell people how to do things, tell them what to do and let them surprise you with their results."
> – *George S. Patton*

Proficiency Level A

"The boss calls it 'follow the leader' but I want to see where we are going!"

- Translates vision into tangible activities for the team.
- Sets clear expectations of what is required.
- Sets priorities and focuses on objectives.
- Shows enthusiasm – pushes others to succeed.
- Leads by example.
- Motivates team by giving praise and encouragement.

> "Making initiatives successful is all about focus and passionate commitment. The drumbeat must be relentless. Every leadership action must demonstrate total commitment to the initiative."
>
> *– Jack Welch*
>
> "Keep away from people who try to belittle your ambitions. Small people always do that, but the really great make you feel that you, too, can become great."
>
> *– Mark Twain*

Case Studies

From the World of Business

1. Jack Welch: The Making of a CEO*

John Francis Welch Jr. (Jack Welch), Chairman and Chief Executive Officer of General Electric Co. (GE), retired after 41 years with GE on September 6, 2001. With his innovative and forceful leadership style as CEO, Jack Welch transformed GE in to a highly productive and efficient company from a lumbering bureaucratic giant.

Jack Welch was, in fact, described as the most important and influential business leader of the 20th century, by several Wall Street analysts and academics. Jack Welch's reputation as a leader could be attributed to four key qualities: he was an intuitive strategist; he was willing to change the rules if necessary; he was highly competitive; and he was a great communicator.

To start at the beginning, Jack Welch got a Ph.D in chemical engineering from the University of Illinois and in 1960, started his career at GE as a Junior Engineer.

However, in 1961, Jack Welch decided to quit his job as he was unhappy with the company's bureaucracy. However, Reuben Gutoff, an executive at GE convinced Jack Welch to stay back. Reuben Gutoff promised that he would prevent him from getting entangled in GE red tape and would create a small-company environment with big-company resources for him. This theme came to dominate Jack Welch's own thinking as the leader of GE. Jack Welch quickly rose to become the head of the Plastics Division in 1968. He became a group executive for the U.S.$1.5 billion Components and Materials group in 1973. This included plastics and GE Medical Systems.

In 1981, Jack Welch became GE's youngest CEO ever. His predecessor, Reg Jones said, "We need entrepreneurs who

---

* Adapted from ICMR cases/caselets; the original versions can be procured from ICMR/accessed on the ICMR website.

are willing to take well-considered business risks and at the same time know how to work in harmony with a larger business entity... The intellectual requirements are light-years beyond the requirements of less complex organisations." In May 1998, *Business Week* had this to say of Welch: "If leadership is an art, then surely Welch has proved himself a master painter."

Jack Welch's Leadership Style

Jack Welch's grasp of what would work best for GE stemmed from knowing the company and those who worked for it. More than half of his time was devoted to people issues. Most importantly, he had created something unique at a big company – **Informality.** The hierarchy was completely changed during his tenure. Everyone, from secretaries, to chauffeurs to factory workers, called him 'Jack'. He gave employees a sense that he knew them and that they were giving their best.

Jack Welch constantly tried to eliminate bureaucracy from the system. He introduced measures such as 'Work-out' and 'Boundaryless Behaviour'. These systems helped GE to become a company where people were curious, open, ever ready to cooperate and always breaking down barriers. Knowing the value of surprise, every week he made unexpected visits to plants and offices. There were luncheons with managers several layers below him, making himself accessible at what he felt was the hands on level also.

Jack figured out that one of the best ingredients of GE's people issues was the reward system and made sure that the best business leaders were rewarded properly. To identify the best, he introduced the concept of 'Vitality Chart'. Using this chart, the employees were sorted as A's, B's and C's. He made sure that GE's best performing employees were being rewarded and recognised. In those early days as the CEO, GE had granted stock option to only 200 employees. Eventually, Jack Welch spread those options throughout large segments of the company and by March 1999, the figure rose to 27,000.

Jack Welch was very focused and analytical. He restructured GE's portfolio from 350 businesses during the 1980s down to around twenty core activities by late 1990s. He expanded internally or made acquisitions to position all GE's businesses as either number one or number two in their fields.

GE under Jack Welch, transformed Six Sigma from a manufacturing quality tool to all service-related transactions. The Six Sigma program increased the company's operating profit margins from 13.6 per cent in 1995 to 16.7 per cent in 1999. Jack attributed three factors to the success of Six Sigma program at GE: aligning employee benefits and promotions with Six Sigma programs; demanding high degree of senior management support to define objectives and facilitate implementation; and working to demonstrate the impact of the Six Sigma initiatives to customers. Jack Welch personally supervised the progress that business units made in their Six Sigma programs.

To promote strategic thinking and planning at GE, Jack Welch introduced the concept of 'Benchmarking', which helped the Operation Executives to address the questions about competitive dynamics like:

- What does your global competitive environment look like?
- In the last three years, what have your competitors done?
- In the same period, what have you done?
- What are your plans to leapfrog them?

During Jack Welch's two decades as CEO, GE grew from a U.S.$13 billion manufacturer of light bulbs and appliances in 1981, into a U.S.$480 billion industrial conglomerate by 2000. Jack Welch had become a 'dealmaking machine', supervising 993 acquisitions worth U.S.$13 billion and selling 408 businesses for a total of about U.S.$10.6 billion.

After stepping down as the CEO, Jack Welch became an advisor to William Harrison, CEO, JP Morgan Chase. As a leadership teacher Jack Welch has left an indelible mark.

> **The Learning**
>
> **Level-C:**
> - Implements systems and processes that promote personal responsibility.
>
> **Level-B:**
> - Creates a clear vision and direction for the business.
>
> **Level-A:**
> - Motivates team by giving praise and encouragement.

Other themes covered: Decision Making, Business focus, Initiative and Proactivity.

2. Mukesh Ambani: Chasing New Frontiers

He discovered one of India's biggest oil and gas fields, managed 100 per cent production from the Jamnagar refinery and carpeted India with 60,000 km of fibre-optic cable. Mukesh Ambani created a top brand in record time and acquired some six million customers in less than one year. Let us look at Mukesh Ambani's successful strategies which made him a name to contend with in the corporate world even as the Ambani empire was split between the two brothers.

When Mukesh Ambani took over as Chairman in July 2002, Reliance's strategy of backward and forward vertical integration had almost run its course. The next big frontier was the opportunities presented by new technology. Mukesh saw the critical role of information, communication and energy increasing in the modern world. He was ready to take the plunge from the word go.

Launched on his father's birthday (28 December 2002), Reliance Infocomm's game plan was not very different from the classic Ambani strategy: straddle the entire value and business chain, build economies of scale, batten down costs, push volumes, drive down prices and offer consumers what they want. Connectivity was to be the bedrock in terms of delivering value across businesses.

The business plan had three elements: a mobile revolution, an enterprise netway revolution; and the third phase would bring about a consumer convergence revolution based on broadband.

Before the revolution flowered, there had to be customers, and the strategy there was 'affordable pricing'. In their revenue model they actually worked backwards by looking at what the customer could afford. Then they worked out what kind of investment would be required to sustain these revenues and make profits. "We also leveraged economies of scale to reduce costs," said Mukesh.

The new focus did not mean less focus on the older petrochemicals business. The acquisitions of ailing companies such as IPCL (2002, at a cost of Rs. 14.91 billion for a 26 per cent stake) and Nocil (2004) have not merely consolidated Reliance's position in the petrochemical industry, but point to the continued emphasis on this sector. Within months of IPCL's takeover, the company staged an impressive turnaround. Mukesh realised that IPCL had several opportunities to grow, through "geographical expansion, market consolidation, acquisitions and green field investments."

Mukesh shares his father's vision to make India, through Reliance, find its place in the world. He sees three major thrust areas. One is technology: how to build cutting edge skills, in terms of enhancing technology, understanding technology, developing technology that will help them stay competitive. The second competency he is strongly focusing on is productivity, both in terms of capital and operations. The third competency he identifies is, customer experience and customer service.

Management Style

Smart leaders seek and cultivate smart followers. As Mukesh Ambani pointed out during a book launch (2000), "India does not need a tie-wallah golf culture. You need leaders at all levels who can drive your company as strong knowledge-based achievers."

In 1981, at age 24, Mukesh joined the family firm. Reliance's sales were Rs 9.4 billion in 1980. Today, it is India's number one private sector company with sales of Rs 657.6 billion and profits close to Rs 48 billion. Its sales represent 3 per cent of India's GDP and its exports of Rs 115 billion are 5 per cent of the country's total export.

So what are Mukesh's core competencies? In an interview with a TV channel, he explained, "I think over the years, Reliance has developed the main competency of building businesses from scratch, of building businesses which it did not know anything about. ...the way we do it is really grow, consolidate, put a separate team to again grow and the cycle continues." The company's global competitiveness is further boosted by a workforce that undergoes continuous skills training.

Mukesh is a manager with the rare ability to see both the big picture and keep track of the small details in which often the profits reside. A meticulous note taker and one who is always organised and well prepared, he holds a formidable reputation as a workaholic. Few people can keep the level of information in their head that Mukesh does with relative ease. He is also a swift executionist. Patalganga, Jamnagar and Infocomm have all been handled speedily. The speed factor gives Reliance huge cost advantages and is a continuation of Dhirubhai's style of management of leading by example.

The Learning

Level-C:
- Implements systems and processes that promote personal responsibility.

Level-B:
- Creates a clear vision and direction for the business.

Level-A:
- Shows enthusiasm – pushes others to succeed.

Other themes covered: Teamwork, Business focus, Initiative and Proactivity.

3. Shahnaz Husain: Pioneer and Leader*

If today Ayurvedic treatment has caught the imagination of the Western countries, the credit goes largely to Shahnaz Husain, the pioneer and leader of herbal care in India. She has achieved unprecedented success and acclaim for her practical application of Ayurveda in beauty care and cosmetics. Belonging to an aristocratic Muslim family, she was married at an early age. She began writing on different subjects including health and beauty when her husband was posted in Tehran.

Later for 10 years she trained in cosmetic therapy and cosmetic chemistry, at leading institutions of the West, like Helena Rubinstein, Arnould Taylor, Swarzkopf, and Lean of Copenhagen. Shahnaz returned to her roots and studied Ayurveda, the ancient Indian system of herbal healing. She was gradually convinced of the superior benefits of Ayurveda and it is then she started thinking of a totally new concept of herbal care and cure. She set up her herbal clinic in her own home, in a very small way, rejecting the existing salon treatment methods and devised her own herbal treatments. She also began to formulate her own Ayurvedic products. The turning point in her business fortunes came when she represented India at the Festival of India in 1980. Her team was given a counter in the perfumery section of the famous Selfridges in London. She managed to sell her entire consignment in 3 days and broke the store's record for cosmetics sales for the year!

This was the beginning of the legendary Shahnaz Herbal and other ranges. In fact, she has become known for her specialised clinical treatments and therapeutic products for a range of problems like acne, pigmentation, scars and blemishes, skin-sensitivity, dandruff, hair loss and alopecia. Today, Shahnaz Husain heads a chain of over 400 franchisee salons in India and abroad, with outlets in prestigious stores and locations all over the world. Her franchise-based enterprise has helped in the worldwide extension of the Shahnaz Herbal clinics, popularising her formidable range of nearly 350 products.

---

* Adapted from ICMR cases/caselets; the original versions can be procured from ICMR/accessed on the ICMR website.

Shahnaz has received several national and international awards, including the *World's Greatest Woman Entrepreneur Award* from Success Group of the U.S.A. She is the first woman to be so honoured in the 107-year history of the Success awards. She has also been honoured with two prestigious international awards for *Quality Excellence* and *Outstanding Woman Entrepreneur 2002*, by Global Quality Management in London. In the year 2006, she received the *Padma Shree* from the then President of India, Dr Abdul Kalam.

Shahnaz Husain is also a pioneer of vocational training in cosmetology in India, having started her professional schools at a time when only apprenticeship training was available.

Shahnaz made, the now famous remark, that she just did not sell herbal beauty care but "a whole civilisation in a jar." She has always looked ahead, towards newer challenges, incorporating the latest techniques and quality control measures. She leads from the front by personal example. She believes in vision and determined hard work. Her natural business instincts and foresight have always led her to the next frontier, and helped her develop an uncanny understanding of future international demands. Her vision transcends geographical boundaries and encompasses the entire world. Indeed, as head of the largest herbal clinic chain of its kind in the world, Shahnaz Husain has become a legend in her own lifetime.

The Learning

Level-C:
- Implements systems and processes that promote personal responsibility.

Level-B:
- Creates a clear vision and direction for the business.

Level-A:
- Shows enthusiasm – pushes others to succeed.

Other themes covered: Business Focus, Initiative and Proactivity, Planning and Organisation

People Development

3. Building Capability

"The boss feels a dog at our heels will build us up quickly for the finals!"

In today's world, which has become more of a global village, most businesses are too complex, wide ranging and fast moving for one manager to be actively involved in every day-to-day decision. To meet the objectives of the organisation, a leader needs to augment the potential of his most important resources i.e., the people.

Once the leader recognises that members of his team want to improve and can perform in extraordinary ways, his next step should be to provide them with opportunities to grow and develop. The benefits this brings out in the organisation are countless.

With this competency:

One develops others to raise the capability of individuals and the team, identifying the proper opportunities for the achievement and enhancement of potential; gathers and gives honest and constructive feedback to subordinates.

LEVELS OF PROFICIENCY
Proficiency Level C

"I trained him too well. I can't take that height myself!"

- Promotes a learning organisation.
- Sets organisational level goals for people development.
- Designs systematic approaches for skills training and staff development.
- Maintains and develops the organisation's intellectual capital.

> "It is literally true that you can succeed best and quickest by helping others to succeed."
> – *Napoleon Hill*
>
> "The world has the habit of making room for the man whose actions show that he knows where he is going."
> – *Napoleon Hill*

Building Capability

Proficiency Level B

"We forgot to tell the boss that he stammers!"

- Identifies professional growth tracks for key resources.
- Creates opportunities for new developmental experiences.
- Identifies challenging processes to develop individuals at all levels.
- Ensures successful transfer of processes or tools and methodologies around the organisation.

"Leaders create an environment in which everyone has the opportunity to do work which matches his potential capability and for which an equitable differential reward is provided."
– *Elliott Jaques*

"What we can or cannot do, what we consider possible or impossible, is rarely a function of our true capability. It is more likely a function of our beliefs about who we are."
– *Anthony Robbins*

Proficiency Level A

"The manager says a good presentation should not have detailed explanations. Facts and figures should be enough!"

- Designs and delivers skills training in a variety of areas.
- Codifies ideas, processes and methods for use by others in the company.
- Provides one-on-one coaching to others to help them modify ineffective behaviour.
- Provides constructive feedback from a range of sources.

> "Practice rather than preach. Make of your life an affirmation, defined by your ideals, not the negation of others. Dare to the level of your capability then go beyond to a higher level."
>
> – *Alexander Haig*

> "The Lord doesn't ask about your ability, only your availability; and, if you prove your dependability, the Lord will increase your capability."
>
> – *Unknown*

Case Studies

From the World of Business

1. Infosys' Institute — Inspiring a New Generation of Leaders*

The founding members of Infosys Technologies Ltd., instilled faith in values and ethical conduct of business. They realised that investors, customers, employees, and vendors had all become more discerning and wanted greater transparency and fairness in all dealings.

Infosys has received many awards for its good governance practices which it imbibed from the beginning. But what of the future? With the idea of building leadership skills, Infosys embarked on a unique project to create what it calls 'quality leaders' with a global perspective. The company has set up the Infosys Leadership Institute (ILI) on a 200-acre stretch of land in Mysore in Karnataka with an investment of $7.3 million. Hereafter, the top management selected employees from the senior level to drivers and peons to undergo training to improve leadership skills and emerge as thought leaders. Nandan Nilekani then CEO, in an interview in 2006, reaffirmed that the institute would help to create intergenerational leaders "and preserve the DNA of the organisation".

The Institute has a team of teachers who inculcate in the students various leadership development elements. The emphasis is on customising training programs to suit the special needs of each participant. However, not every employee can go for leadership training at the institute. ILI management has put in place a rigorous system to select the right Infoscians to be trained. Department heads are asked to appraise employees by benchmarking them with some of the best core competencies practiced in some of the world's best managed companies. Those who possess the best traits of leadership are then selected to embark on the training

---

* Adapted from ICMR cases/caselets; the original versions can be procured from ICMR/accessed on the ICMR website.

sessions in Mysore. The training program offers courses on developmental relationships, sharing and transfer of knowledge, creating a bond between one another, and inculcating Infosys culture and community empathy.

ILI is the first such institute that an Indian company has come up with. The institute concept came from Narayana Murthy, who is credited with setting new standards in work culture and employee-employer relations in India's corporate history. Now many other orgnisations have developed their own training facilities.

Expounding his theory of leadership, Narayana Murthy said in answer to an India Abroad query, "A true leader is one who leads by example and sacrifices more than anyone else in his or her pursuit of excellence. It is our vision at Infosys to create world-class leaders who will be at the forefront of business and technology in today's competitive marketplace". He said the institute was launched, "to instill in our employees creativity, to bring new ideas to fruition, make transition to new paradigms, and embrace change…"

The Learning

Level-C:
- Promotes a learning organisation.

Level-B:
- Creates a clear vision and direction for the business.

Level-A:
- Designs and delivers skills/training in a variety of areas.

Other themes covered: Leadership

2. The Taj's People Philosophy*

The Taj Group of Hotels is run by IHCL, a part of the Tata Group. The Taj Group had always believed that their employees were their greatest assets and the very reason for the survival of their business. According to a senior Taj official: "Talent management is the most important sustainable competitive advantage for future growth." The employee at Taj is viewed as an asset and is 'the real profit centre'.

In 2000, to show its commitment to and belief in employees, the Taj Group developed the *Taj People Philosophy* (TPP), which covered all the people practices of the group. TPP considered every aspect of the employees' organisational career planning, right from their induction into the company till their superannuation.

In March 2001, the Taj Group launched an employee loyalty program called the *Special Thanks and Recognition System* (STARS). This was an initiative aimed at motivating employees to transcend their usual duties and responsibilities and have fun during work. This program also acknowledged and rewarded hard working employees who had done excellent work.

It helped the company boost the morale of its employees and improve service standards, which in turn resulted in repeat customers for many hotels in the group. The STAR system also led to global recognition of the Taj Group of hotels in 2002 when the group bagged the *Hermes Award* for *Best Innovation in Human Resources* in the global hospitality industry.

Since its establishment, the Taj Group had a people-oriented culture. The group always hired fresh graduates from leading hotel management institutes all over India so that it could shape their attitudes and develop their skills in a way that fitted its needs and culture. The management wanted the new recruits to pursue a long-term career with the group. All new employees were placed in an intensive two-year training program, which familiarised them with the business ethos of the group, the management practices of the organisation and the working of cross-functional departments.

---

* Adapted from ICMR cases/caselets; the original versions can be procured from ICMR/accessed on the ICMR website.

The employees of the Taj Group were trained in varied fields like sales and marketing, finance, hospitality and service, front office management and food and beverages etc. They also had to participate in various leadership programs so that they could develop in them a strong, warm and professional work culture. Through these programs, the group was able to assess the future potential of the employees and the training required to further develop their skills. The group offered excellent opportunities to employees both on personal as well as the organisational front. The group strove hard to standardize all its processes and evolve a work culture which appealed to all its employees universally.

The STAR campaign offers no cash awards. Recognition comes in the form of levels. Points can be picked up by employees for integrity, reliability, outstanding work, courage of conviction and initiative. Practical and useful suggestions that are beneficial to the company can also earn an employee points. Says HR vice president, "Many employees do that extra bit, go out of the way to dazzle the customer... It is based on the premise that happy employees lead to happy customers." However, while employees can earn merit points for acts of excellence or valuable suggestions, one can also earn 20 'default merit' points. There are five recognition levels with varying number of points to be earned. After the campaign was launched, a large number of employees started working together in the true team spirit.

The Taj HR model has been adopted as a case study by the renowned Harvard Business School since 2002.

The Learning

Level-C:
- Designs systematic approaches for skills training and staff development.

Level-B:
- Identifies challenging processes to develop individuals at all levels.

Other themes covered: Leadership, Continuous Improvement, Innovation.

3. Pramod Chaudhari: Hands-on Learning*

Praj Industries Ltd., Pune established in 1984 began with supplying alcohol and brewery plants and equipment from concept to commissioning, as well as fruit processing plants. Today it is a global company, providing the latest solutions for distillery and brewery waste water treatment and utilisation. Pramod Chaudhari (58 yrs) founder chairman and managing director, is a perfect example of a manager-turned entrepreneur, who preferred to learn the basics the hard way.

A graduate in mechanical engineering from IIT Mumbai, Pramod Chaudhari joined Bajaj Tempo in 1971 as a trainee and by choice worked on the shop floor. This was uncommon; most engineers are unwilling to sweat it out on the shop floor with workers or soil their hands even to acquire real experience. Pramod wanted to see how workers actually worked with their hands and tried it out himself. "It was hands-down learning... I made the choice because I considered it *necessary grounding* for becoming a real manager of men and machines."[1]

Pramod wanted to gain experience in sales and service. So he moved to Widia where he sharpened his commercial negotiation skills in specific aspects like contract negotiation, payment terms, convincing the customer and market development. He acquired leadership skills by getting the engineering staff to adhere to stringent work norms. Pramod developed a sharp achievers instinct and proficiency in closing deals.

At Widia, his engineering background combined with his shopfloor experience proved invaluable. Pramod says of those days: "Telco was a major battleground for us in Widia. Jakatdar, their MD was a visionary, who was bringing in modern technology in machining. He relied on Widia for their

---

* Reproduced with permission, ©McGraw Hill Education, India, B4, Sector 63, Dist. Gautam Budh Nagar, Noida, U.P. 201301.

[1] *Thought Leaders: The Source Code of Exceptional Managers and Entrepreneurs* by Shrinivas Pandit. Tata McGraw-Hill Publishing Company Limited, New Delhi, 2002 (reprint) p.40.

every need. So, special tooling was becoming a major issue."[2] Pramod's advantage was that he could stand by the product and demonstrate it personally, whereas the Sandvik person had to take an assistant with him. He was able to mix freely with workers, machine tool design engineers, managers and talk in their language and convince them. Thus, a relationship grew with Telco due to technical competence and deft handling of human relations.

Later Pramod took his own path and set up Praj in 1984. He managed to get the necessary permissions through his own persuasive ways. No bribes were paid; there was no previous connection or any recommendation letter. They could not help but respond to his sincerity of purpose. How did he impress them?

Pramod recalls, "I approached them up-front and impressed them with my straight dealing. I would dash off to Delhi or wherever. I presented exhaustive technical data. I used techno-commercial language to convince them. I gave them clarity of thought, an IIT background, and I was very persuasive; but above all, the substance of our proposal was appealing."[3] Pramod convinced people that he wanted to create a technologically-effective, better-engineered plant in contrast to the traditionally manufactured and technically weak plants. Pramod provided a better economic package with lower capital costs and cost of production along with other benefits to the mills. He created an image of a professional team on the basis of his approach and he could relate better because of his rural background. He got the permission.

Pramod lays great emphasis on execution. He understands that 'God is in the details' as they say. Any plan needs an equally strong execution. Today, they have a corpus of good orders and a strategy in place. The organisation has a good market spread and a strong brand name. The way they execute the plan or the orders is what will make a difference to their future growth. Having realised this very early on, they took care to understand the nuances of

---

[2] Ibid. p.43.
[3] Ibid. p.45.

executing the quantum. And they are out to further augment their execution strength. Praj has planned two other manufacturing bases and as a long-term resourcing policy, a base near the port which will reduce the time to market.

Pramod is clear about his goals. Great diversity or sheer size is not the most important factor. Praj Industries as an organisation has to be internationally recognised for the quality supply of alcohol and brewery plant and equipment, with service that satisfies the customer.

The Learning

Level-C:
- Maintains and develops the organisation's intellectual capital.

Level-B:
- Creates opportunities for new developmental experiences.

Other themes covered: Leadership.

Work Effectiveness

1. Analytical Skills

"All the data we have collected boss, points to one thing. This is risky business!"

Analysis is the process by which you understand the whole of something by breaking it down into parts. By understanding its components and how they fit together in a large whole, you understand the full picture better. The various ways that you can break things down into parts and then use those parts to understand the original thing or other things are called analytical skills and every case you take will teach you various types of analytical skills.

With this competency:

One identifies problems to be addressed; collects suitable and relevant data and analyses data in a systematic way; generates effective countermeasures to solve the problem; and remains focused.

LEVELS OF PROFICIENCY
Proficiency Level C

"Ha! Ha! I have finally got a model which only I can explain!"

- Sees relationships in seemingly unrelated data.
- Creates models and processes to solve complex problems.
- Shows lateral thinking and creative vision in addressing complex problems.
- Works with partial or conflicting complex data to identify key issues.
- Understands medium- and long-term impact of problems/solutions on people and organisational processes.

> "What is out there? What leads to what? What makes things happen? And what is controllable? These concerns underlie the scientists search for knowledge, the artist's search for creation, the philosopher's search for truth, and the exceptional manager's search for excellence."
> – *Michael Schulman*
> The Passionate Mind

Proficiency Level B

"Look here, I am the consultant hired to identify your emotional issues. I can't resolve them!"

- Anticipates need for information to resolve issues.
- Identifies and gathers relevant information from a range of different sources and perspectives.
- Considers people and emotional issues in analysis.
- Recognises themes and trends within data.
- Identifies key issues.
- Develops hypothesis and tests them out.
- Stands back to gain an overview of the information.
- Identifies the pro's and con's of different options.
- Considers longer term implications of data.
- Able to apply a general principle and common standards to a specific situation.

> "The 'I' in India should not stand for imitation or inhibition. It must stand for innovation."
> – *Raghunath Mashelkar*
>
> "Behind every successful brand, there is an exceptional executive."
> – *Shrinivas Pandit*
> Thought Leaders

Analytical Skills

Proficiency Level A

"I am testing out this hypnosis tool which can direct customers to the right products?"

- Uses past experience to predict future issues.
- Undertakes research to gain information.
- Gains sufficient data to reach a decision without getting bogged down in detail.
- Does not make assumptions and clarifies what others don't understand.
- Breaks problems into logical chunks; cross-checks across the problem.
- Uses funnelling process to arrive at the root of the problem.
- Spots gaps in data.

> "Remember, it is neither a formula for success nor an atmosphere congenial to growth which alone matters. It is the alchemical drive to attain great heights in one's chosen domain which counts."
> – ***Shrinivas Pandit***
>   Thought Leaders

Case Studies

From the World of Business

1. Raghunath Mashelkar: A Leader and Scientist*

Raghunath Mashelkar is a renowned polymer scientist who has made original contributions in diverse areas, from polymer science to engineering. He has 220 research publications, 18 books and 24 patents to his credit. As the head of Council for Scientific and Industrial Research (CSIR), he left a deep impact on the organisation. Mashelkar's analytical skills – especially the way he collected suitable and relevant data, analysed it and generated effective countermeasures to solve problems, helped him throughout his career to become almost a legend. He also was able to see the medium- and long-term results of a set of actions like most visionaries.

Mashelkar realised that the use of turmeric to heal wounds has been known in India for centuries. He had first seen its application at home as a child. This triggered him off to challenge the U.S. patents and trademark office. With his team of researchers, he decided to collect every possible piece of information and collate it. He even got some old Sanskrit texts translated into English and pulled out references from history.

When all the information was collected and the evidence seemed convincing, he coordinated the case between the Ministries of Agriculture, Environment and External Affairs to launch an offensive in the U.S..

The verdict was passed in India's favour. The determining factor for the success was that the case was well researched and articulated, legally and sensitively. Thorough preparation was the key. The case complete with data, figures and facts sequenced in logically, led to success. Mashelkar always believed that glib talk never helps. One needs to present cold facts in a lucid style in the language of the receiver.

---

* Reproduced with permission, ©McGraw Hill Education, India, B4, Sector 63, Dist. Gautam Budh Nagar, Noida, U.P. 201301.

Analytical Skills 91

Mashelkar's 'patent, publish, prosper' drive and its turmeric patent victory, gave CSIR a massive boost. Evaluating his victory that was more of India's triumph, he said, "Of course, it was a matter of great pride for us all. This was the first time that from the third world there was a challenge thrown to the U.S. patents and trademarks office, on a patent given on the traditional knowledge of India."[1]

The Learning

Level-C:
- Understands medium- and long-term impact of problems/solutions on people and organisational processes.

Level-B:
- Identifies and gathers relevant information from a range of different sources and perspectives.

Level-A:
- Undertakes research to gain information.

Other themes covered: Leadership, Planning and Organising

2. The Case of AMWAY

No problem can be solved without proper analysis of the issue. This is true for all levels. There is a lot to learn from the experiences of the leading global direct marketing major – Amway, and the way they took on the countermeasures in India to tackle a host of problems.

Amway's dream of a successful launch in India had gone astray from the very first day. Though the company managed to rope in a substantial number of distributors, the attrition rate was at an alarming high of 60-65 per cent.

Amway soon woke up to the reality that it had to take steps to put its Multilevel Marketing machinery back on

---

[1] *Thought Leaders: The Source Code of Exceptional Managers and Entrepreneurs* by Shrinivas Pandit. Tata McGraw-Hill Publishing Company Limited, New Delhi, 2002 (reprint) p. 181

track. But first, it had to identify what had gone wrong. Why had things not worked?

Firstly, Amway was burdened with an image that its products were expensive. But the reality was that Amway's products were highly concentrated and made for a long shelf-life. For instance, the product named LOC (priced above Rs 320 for a 1-litre pack) when diluted gave around 165 bottles. The cost per usage was thus very low. As the distributors were unable to communicate this to the user, Amway started putting stickers on its products, which clearly indicated the number of usages per bottle.

Amway realised that a complicated market like India needed a focused approach for each of the product categories. To strengthen its product focus, Amway set up strategic business units and appointed category managers for individual product categories.

The company also decided to give incentives to clearing and forwarding agents who could deliver parcels in the same city within 48 hours and outside within 72 hours.

Amway then took two critical steps. It tapped unemployed youth in smaller towns by subsidising the entry fee for the starters sales kit. Then it also started giving interest-free loans to finance these kits. It even gave free kits to visually impaired youth in Rajasthan.

In a bid to make its products more affordable, Amway introduced value-for-money 'chhota (small) packs' in December 1999. The sachets significantly boosted sales. Sachets had two advantages – they helped Amway shake off the 'super-premium-products-only' tag and with their low prices, invited consumers from lower income levels to try the products.

All these measures helped Amway to overcome the troubles it faced at the start and strengthen its roots in India.

Analytical Skills

> **The Learning**
>
> *Level-C:*
> - Creates models and processes to solve complex problems.
>
> *Level-B:*
> - Identifies key issues.
>
> *Level-A:*
> - Breaks problems into logical chunks; cross-checks across the problem.

Other themes covered: Leadership, Planning and Organising, Managing Change.

3. Verghese Kurien: Strategic Leadership*

Verghese Kurien needs no introduction. He is to the white revolution what Dr M. S. Swaminathan is to the green. Dr Kurien has always been a fighter and negotiator par excellence, ready to take on tough adversaries, relying on self-confidence and strategic planning. He is a master of backing arguments with facts and figures and plans every move well in advance, keeping his ace cards close to his chest till the time they are required. He goes to the root cause with analysis. One battle he took up was against poor quality food aid to India.

The battle against the delivery of unusable commodities had raged between 1970 and 1973; the government's protests and pleas were ignored. The transmitting agency, WFP's failure to maintain quality and the continuous inflow of food aid under Operation Flood also lengthened the duration of the first phase itself to eleven years. The delay caused a reduction in investments in a series of technical programmes and the conduct of the entire sequence of Operation Flood had become very difficult for Kurien. At the 20th International Dairy Congress held in Paris in June 1978, Kurien castigated them. He spoke of his own intervention thus: "When we

---

* Reproduced with permission, ©McGraw Hill Education, India, B4, Sector 63, Dist. Gautam Budh Nagar, Noida, U.P. 201301.

complained, we were in effect told that beggars could not be choosers. And, finally, when I had to intervene in the matter, I simply had to reject the commodities in question and declare that India was not a dumping ground for commodities unfit for human consumption. Surely, it should not have been necessary for me to say that?"

"The fact of the matter is, that the agencies are often much more closely identified with the donors than they are with the recipients. They hold out their hands to the donors and accept whatever crumbs may fall from the table, instead of representing the recipients and insisting that moral commitments be adhered to. We are not supplicants. We are not beggars. And, I submit, the donors are not doing us any favour." Ruth Heredia, in her book *The Amul Story of India*, states that never before had a delegate from a developing country spoken quite so frankly in that forum. "The facts were incontrovertible. But he had to accept as an inevitable consequence the envy and malevolence of many."

Kurien fought with institutions manned by different nationalities and often in a foreign land. Wherever there was a bottleneck, Kurien rushed in to remove, circumvent or demolish it. What Kurien did was to demolish psychological fortifications with an abundant supply of facts. He first disarmed the western adversaries in their favourite obsession of playing with facts, information and data. When they became exposed and vulnerable, the focus shifted to intentions. It was a battle of wits which Kurien won with his ability to gather and analyse information and using it to fight for causes he believed in.

The speeches are flooded with facts, data, convincing arguments and pearls of wisdom. There is a fervent appeal to one's conscience. Kurien's mastery of macro-level issues and their impact on micro-level cooperative institutions is breathtaking. Decades after Kurien's rise to fame, the tenet on participatory development that he propounded became a byword.

Kurien is multiskilled. He has networking and drafting skills and is highly articulate. On being asked what he

Analytical Skills

considered the most critical skills, he underscored four points:
- Where you have the will you will have the skills;
- Study, search, practice, application;
- Healthy irreverence;
- Look for the kink in the thing, be curious.

The Learning

Level-C:
- Creates an environment that promotes ownership and accountability at all levels.

Level-B:
- Creates a clear vision and direction for the business

Level-A:
- Translates vision into tangible activities for the team

Other themes covered: Leadership.

Work Effectiveness

2. Decision Making

"What do we do now sir? The number of pros and cons are equal!!"

It is not easy to define decision making. It is the process of sufficiently reducing uncertainty and doubt about alternatives to allow a reasonable choice to be made. This definition stresses the information-gathering function of decision making. It should be noted here that, uncertainty is *reduced* rather than eliminated. Very few decisions are made with absolute certainty because complete knowledge about all the alternatives is seldom possible. Thus, every decision involves a certain amount of risk. This is true both for our professional as also our personal lives.

With this competency:

One weighs up the pros and cons of different options; all relevant factors are considered when making decisions; prepared to make decisions, involving others as appropriate.

LEVELS OF PROFICIENCY

Proficiency Level C

"That's the boss showing us how good he is in 'tightrope walking'."

- Collects information from different sources to evaluate the situation and reach the right decision.
- Is able to help others reach decisions within deadlines.
- Takes risk-mitigation measures and encourages others to take risks in a controlled manner.
- Anticipates the need for decisions in different areas/functions.
- Able to foresee the impact of other's decisions on self and plan accordingly.

> "Choose always the way that seems the best, however rough it may be. Custom will soon render it easy and agreeable."
> – *Pythagoras*

> "Information is a source of learning. But unless it is organised, processed, and available to the right people in a format for decision making, it is a burden, not a benefit."
> – *William Pollard*

Proficiency Level B

"You served tea in the executive board meeting. Tell me, what was the reaction to my presentation?"

- Anticipates the need for decisions in own area.
- Seeks information from conventional and non-conventional sources.
- Uses all formal and informal channels to get the required information.
- Considers the impact of the decision on different areas.
- Considers risk-reward scenarios and may take higher risks at the appropriate time.

> "Informed decision making comes from a long tradition of guessing and then blaming others for inadequate results."
> – *Scott Adams*
>
> "Find ways to decentralise. Move decision making authority down and out. Encourage a more entrepreneurial approach."
> – *Donald Rumsfeld*

Proficiency Level A

"He is running to take the majority opinion among the staff, Sir. We take a decision in 10 minutes!"

- Plans to be able to reach a decision within the required timeframe.
- Involves people within own area in making decision to create ownership.
- Understands the need to make timely decisions.
- Seeks information from all conventional sources to arrive at a decision.

> "Intuitive decision making and mastering this profession are one and the same."
> – *Unknown*
>
> "We need to constantly update our skills and levels of awareness about the changing realities at the ground level."
> – *Dr. Amrita Patel*

Case Studies

From the World of Business

1. Vision Behind Small Car – Nano

In early January 2008, the Nano was unveiled by Ratan Tata, chairman of Tata group at the Auto Expo in New Delhi. This attracted great media attention and unexpectedly was followed by similar plan announcements by other players within a few days.

When Ratan Tata had first broached the subject with his managers, it had created anxiety, ridicule, and disbelief. How could a car in these expensive times be made for a cost as low as Rs. 100,000 and why should Tata Motors take on such an incredible project, just because the figure had practically slipped out of the chairman's mouth! Later on, of course, industry circles have come to realise that Ratan Tata always had a deeper vision when he talked of a small affordable car for the common man. This vision was not driven merely by the picture of family of four riding a scooter on busy roads; Ratan Tata's decision to go ahead and face all the risks was not due to a romantic idea or emotional outburst. No wonder he followed the big day with several interviews to the media on questions of environmental pollution, pricing, and corporate responsibilities. He agreed that it could set off a trend, but it was essentially biting off the two-wheeler market and not so much the small car segment.

Ratan Tata also tried to explain his entrepreneurial vision, which was mainly responsible for his taking such a decision, despite a lot of teething problems. The way Nano will be built and sold is going to be very different from the way others cars are brought to the showroom. One financial paper calls it the 'Mc Donaldisation of the car industry', but Tata wants the small guy to help him assemble and sell the car. This way, he hopes to create new business opportunities for young engineers across the nation, even while finding a cost-effective way to take Nano to the remotest corners of the market.

"We would create entrepreneurs across the country over time that could produce the same car," the Tata group chairman told the *Economic Times* in an exclusive interview. "We would produce all the mass items and ship it to them as kits so it is similar to an SKD or CKD operation." he explained.

The company plans to bring together business aspirants from around the nation to set up satellite assembling and dealership operations. These entrepreneurs need not have experience in the automobile industry. "My aim was that, we would produce a certain volume of cars and then I would create a very low-cost, low-break-even plant that a young entrepreneur could buy and that a bunch of young entrepreneurs could establish an assembly operation in," Ratan Tata said in an interview. Tata Motors would retain the responsibility for quality assurance and in training people, who will oversee the operations of these entrepreneurs. The whole subsystem will look up to the manufacturing strengths of Tata Motors but will do final assembly at the local units. Thus, Ratan Tata had worked out even a business model and the nuts and bolts of an action plan before he decided to go ahead firmly on his dream car for people.

The Learning

Level-C:
- Takes risk-mitigation measures and encourages others to take risks in a controlled manner.

Level-B:
- Uses all formal and informal channels to get the required information.

Level-A:
- Understands the need to make timely decisions.

Other themes covered: Influence and Negotiation, Initiative and Proactivity.

2. Naveen Jindal: Seeing the Bigger Picture

Naveen Jindal faced a serious challenge at a young age. When he took over the reigns of the Raigarh operations of the Jindal organisation, the company was making losses and lacked proper direction. Ever ready to take calculated risks, he decided that they needed to pursue innovative approaches and optimise operational efficiencies.

Sponge iron was the backbone of the Raigarh operations. After studying the scenario, one of the first decisions he took was to bring global economies of scale in their sponge iron production. Today, Naveen Jindal can proudly say that they have the largest coal-based sponge iron manufacturing capacity in the world and are one of the lowest cost producers of sponge iron.

At the same time, he also realised that affecting reduction in costs was the guideline for long-term growth and profitability. At Raigarh, the commissioning of the new blast furnace he realised would not only enhance their steel-making capacities but also reduce their costs of production. And continuing the path of forward integration, he took the decision to set up the Rail and Universal Beam mill, which is manufacturing the world's longest rails in the country and also parallel flange beams and columns in larger sizes for the first time in India. This helped them gain entry in the highly competitive global markets.

Realising the need to reduce inventory costs and be able to market their finished products at competitive prices, Naveen took the decision to acquire coal and iron ore mines. This made Jindal self-sufficient in key raw materials, essential for steel manufacture. This business model of complete backward and forward integration has become a benchmark in the steel industry.

The company was identified as one of the top emerging companies in the country by India's leading economic newspaper, *The Economic Times* and as the top twenty investor friendly companies in the year 2004 by *Business Today*. At Raigarh, the company is achieving economies of scale that are increasingly making Jindal Steel the preferred choice with the customers. The Company continues to seek new horizons that complement the market strengths, offer growth potential and leverage their existing assets for future growth and expansion.

As a good corporate citizen, Naveen is equally committed to the upliftment and improving the lot of the underprivileged and is determined to do his best for their all-round development.

He has already taken up the task of improving the conditions in 42 villages that have been adopted. The key issues have been identified and continuous efforts are being made to bring about changes in their environment. From better sewage systems and construction of highways to novel education schemes; from women's welfare programs to safe drinking water. Medical camps are organised thrice every week.

Naveen Jindal hit the headlines in 2002 when he won a case in the Supreme Court to fly the Indian flag in private buildings. His dogged pursuit of what he believed to be right is one more example of his perseverance and strong desire to win.

The Learning

Level-C:
- Collects information from different sources to evaluate the situation and reach the right decision.

Level-B:
- Considers risk/reward scenarios and may take higher risks at the appropriate time.

Other themes covered: Leadership, Initiative and Proactivity.

3. Sunil Mittal: Business Focus par Excellence

Sunil Mittal is one of the greatest business leaders of contemporary India. Mittal is the Chairman and the Managing Director of Bharti Airtel Ltd., Bharti India's leading private integrated Telecom Company. Its services include, mobile communication services, telephone services, Broadband services, wireless internet services and services for business enterprises.

Sunil Mittal started his career immediately after graduation from Punjab University. He started out in business at a very young age by making cycle parts in Ludhiana in the Punjab during the 1970s. This was not big enough for him. Later, he moved to Delhi in 1981 and seeing the opportunity went into business of importing and distribution of portable generators from Japan. This business also stopped following a government ban on import of generators.

Later, he introduced push button phones, cordless phones, answering machines and fax machines to India. He was among the first entrepreneurs to be a part of the mobile telecom business in India. In 1995, he launched cellular services in the city of Delhi.

Today, Bharti Airtel has the largest customer base in India with alliances with companies such as Vodafone and SingTel. In the future, his expansion plans include providing international mobile services, retail industry and agriculture. He recently struck a joint venture deal with Wal-Mart – the retail giant, for starting retail stores across India. That Reliance is one of his main rivals in both cellular services and retail, does not deter him. But when Reliance first announced its plans to enter the telecom business with CDMA technology, Mittal went through a period of uncertainty and doubt. The GSM operators were in for trouble. At a meeting of his senior management in Agra, he told them that it was best to lie low and ride out the crisis. They did not make any public announcements and went about their business quietly.

And that made history.[1] The Reliance group entered their arena but did not make a dent on their business.

Talking at an IBM Leadership Group Forum in April 2006, Sunil Mittal outlined the major challenges that Bharti faced over the last few years. He was clear that with India's annual per capita income only a bit over $600, cellular phone service had to be provided for the Indian market at a very low price, perhaps less than two cents a minute. The only way to provide telecom services so inexpensively and run a profitable business, was to take advantage of India's large population and economic growth, scaling up the business rapidly by adding substantively to the customer base every month.

For this, Sunil Mittal had to develop a radically innovative business model, focus only on the customers and outsource just about everything else. In other words, put all the energy of the business into attracting, supporting and retaining customers and accept the fact that almost everything else has been commoditised and should be outsourced, including managing all the IT equipment and the network. Naturally, there was a lot of resistance to this strategy from professionals and even family. People from around the world expressed apprehension and said that IT and the network were the heart of a telecom company. How could one do business by sourcing out the core?

Mittal did not agree and insisted that the customer not the technology, was at the core of his business and then proceeded to implement his strategy. He further surprised everyone by ignoring Indian companies as his outsourcing partners and instead choosing IBM to run IT and Nokia and Ericsson to run the network. He went for highly experienced international companies that could keep up with the punishing pace of Bharti's growth. Sunil Mittal was always confident that his speed in decision making and execution was a core strength and could not be matched by other big groups. Today, Bharti is one of the top five companies in India, and Mittal's vision for it is to be India's most admired brand by 2010.

---

[1] *Men of Steel* . . . op. cit. p.28.

> **The Learning**
>
> *Level-C:*
> - Takes risk-mitigation measures and encourages others to take risks in a controlled manner.
>
> *Level-B:*
> - Considers risk-reward scenarios and may take higher risks at the appropriate time.
>
> *Level-A:*
> - Understands the need to make timely decisions.

Other themes covered: Planning and Organising, Leadership, Personal Responsibility.

Work Effectiveness

3. Planning and Organising

"Where is the main plan? These are all contingencies!"

Every organisation like an individual needs to plan, prioritise and organise. Why? The future is uncertain. Everybody needs to plan and organise his/her future course of actions so that there is a clear path to pursue. In order to be better prepared for change, one has to build contingencies for the uncertain events that may occur in the future. What happens when we don't plan out our future activities? The whole workflow comes to a halt; there is chaos and panic at the workplace.

With this competency:

One establishes (sets) priorities and develops a clear, efficient and logical plan, scheduling to achieve goals; anticipates potential problems and likely contingencies and tries to address them; monitors progress against objectives and takes action to ensure that deadline and outcome/goals are achieved; sets priorities with a clear, logical plan to achieve goals.

Levels of Proficiency
Proficiency Level C

"Come on! don't be nervous. I want your honest feedback immediately!"

- Builds the most effective action plans for reaching organisational goals.
- Controls the execution of plans and uses feedback to improve performance.
- Plans and manages own time to maximize efficiency and other people's time.
- Creates plans for different projects, at the same time re-scoping and defining deliverables, while meeting deadlines and objectives. Estimates time required to complete a job.

> "He who fails to plan, plans to fail."
> – *Proverb*
>
> "Planning is bringing the future into the present so that you can do something about it now."
> – *Alan Lakein*
>
> "A good plan today is better than a perfect plan tomorrow."
> – *Proverb*
>
> "Let our advance worrying become advance thinking and planning."
> – *Winston Churchill*

Proficiency Level B

"This is no fancy dress party, Sir. It's our fall back plan in case of a terrorist attack!"

- Forward thinking – considers long-term issues in plans.
- Aware of time differences when planning.
- Builds contingencies into plans and fall-back position.
- Identifies systems and methods for self and others.
- Uses formal planning methods and tools.

> "When planning for a year, plant corn. When planning for a decade, plant trees. When planning for life, train and educate people."
> – *Chinese Proverb*
>
> "It pays to plan ahead. It wasn't raining when Noah built the ark."
> – *Proverb*
>
> "Unless commitment is made, there are only promises and hopes; but no plans."
> – *Peter F. Drucker*

Proficiency Level A

"You three will share one room. Learn to be a team, before you take charge of your own separate units!"

- Breaks task down into a series of manageable steps.
- Maintains focus on end objective.
- Ensures project is on track.
- Plans at an appropriate level of detail.
- Creates plans which meet timescales and deadlines.
- Anticipates potential problems.
- Builds communication strategy into planning.
- Logs progress and feedback project status.

> "For every minute spent in organising, an hour is earned."
> – *A. A. Milne*

> "The trouble with organising a thing is that pretty soon folks get to paying more attention to the organisation than to what they're organised for."
> – *Laura Ingalls Wilder*

> "In this world no one rules by love; if you are but amiable, you are no hero; to be powerful, you must be strong, and to have dominion you must have a genius for organising."
> – *John Henry Newman*

Case Studies

From the World of Business

1. The GE Workout: The Bottom-up Approach*

GE was a large organisation with several hierarchical layers that promoted bureaucracy and delay in decision making. Jack Welch was deeply concerned about cutting out delays and improving teamwork. The Workout thought came to his mind as he tried to visualise a suitable forum that would enhance teamwork. As the name suggests, the idea was to take the unnecessary work out of the system. But the big question was, "How to achieve this?" The success of the whole GE Workout exercise can be attributed to one single factor – Planning and Organising. Jack made a very comprehensive plan to implement this.

First of all, he wanted to create an open atmosphere in all the business of GE. For this he suggested that business leaders couldn't run the workout sessions. He brought trained facilitators from outside to take the session.

Around 50-100 employees would attend a work-out session to share views on the business and bureaucracy that hindered their work. Jack also planned that every business unit would have to hold hundreds of workouts.

The following schedule was organised: The workout would start with a presentation by the manager, who might outline a broad agenda and then leave. Without the boss present and with a facilitator to move the discussions, employees were asked to list problems, debate solutions and be prepared to sell their ideas when the boss returned. The facilitator helped to make the exchanges between the employees and the manager go a lot easier.

The managers had to make on-the-spot Yes or No decisions on at least 75 per cent of the proposals. If a decision was not made on the spot, there would be an agreed-upon date for a

---

* Adapted from ICMR cases/caselets; the original versions can be procured from ICMR/accessed on the ICMR website.

decision. No proposal would be ignored. The idea was those closest to the function should suggest ways to improve and reach organisational goals.

The workout exercise turned out to be a success. By mid 1992, more than 2,00,000 GE employees had been involved in workouts. Jack Welch's workout concept went on to become a standard module for aligning teamwork with business goals of the organisation.

The Learning

Level-C:
- Builds the most effective action plans for reaching organisational goals.
- Controls the execution of plans and uses feedback to improve performance.

Level-B:
- Forward thinking – considers long-term issues in plans.

Level-A:
- Maintains focus on end objective.

Other themes covered: Leadership, Communication.

2. The Frooti Re-launch*

Frooti had always been positioned as a drink for children. Owing to stagnating sales, Parle Agro planned to re-launch 'Frooti' by re-positioning it.

Now, the management wanted to re-position the drink for the youth, the college-going teenagers. It was a big task as very accurate planning was required; it was a delicate job that could, with one false step, knock off the brand from the market.

The management launched a teaser campaign. As a part of creating hype around the product, a mysterious character called "Digen Verma" was created and introduced to the

---

* Adapted from ICMR cases/caselets; the original versions can be procured from ICMR/accessed on the ICMR website.

public. The objective was clear in the mind – to showcase the rebellious spirit of the youth represented by Digen Verma.

The campaign was very well designed. It used all available channels of communication. The advertisement was aimed to create curiosity among the masses and bring the character to life. Posters at the bus stop asked, "will Digen Verma be in the next bus?" In movie halls, a sudden interruption read, "Digen, your car is being towed." In the car park area, almost all the cars had stickers on them saying, "Digen Verma was here."

The creative management team of Everest Integrated Communications, in charge of the campaign studied in detail the typical modern youth; where the typical college goers hung out; what their reference points were and what would grab their attention.

The team faced many issues that needed sound planning and execution. First, the name of the brand ambassador had to be a ubiquitous one. Second, this fictitious character was to lead a life that normal consumers could relate to. Finally, the storyline had to be powerful enough to sustain interest.

The name 'Digen Verma' was chosen because though it was unusual, yet it was not uncommon. Also, the surname Verma featured in almost all Indian communities. On the other hand, Digen as such didn't mean anything.

Once the name was chosen, the personality had to be built around it. He had to be some sort of a role model whom others would want to imitate. The creative team did not choose any celebrity because he felt that a celebrity's life is always shortlived. That's how the idea of Digen Verma came into the picture – a common man.

A very creative promotional campaign was required, which could communicate its intended position and differentiate it from its competitors. An aggressive multimedia advertising campaign was rolled out across the nation. The campaign included TV commercials, outdoor media campaign, offline promotions and online advertising campaigns, all within a shoestring budget.

Many interesting stories about Digen Verma and his identity started doing the rounds. The enigma called 'Digen

Verma' was everywhere; in buses, in movie halls, colleges and shopping malls.

The frooti tetrapak was given a new packaging. New 'Splash' graphics were introduced on the pack with a flip top packaging replacing the aperture for a straw. The tagline was changed to 'just like that' from the previous 'juice up your life' and 'fresh and juicy.'

The 'Digen Verma' promotion campaign was one of the best designed and innovative teaser campaigns ever made in India. The campaign was able to generate tremendous interest. Though it cost about Rs 30 million, the attention it captured was quite phenomenal. Within a short time after the campaign was launched, the sales went up by almost 30 per cent.

The Learning

Level-C:
- Controls the execution of plans and uses feedback to improve performance.
- Builds the most effective action plans for reaching organisational goals.

Level-B:
- Uses formal planning methods and tools.
- Forward thinking – considers long-term issues in plans.

Level-A:
- Builds communication strategy into planning.
- Anticipates potential problems.

Other themes covered: Communication, Business Focus.

Achieving Business Results

1. Business Focus

"Hurry up man, I am the boss and not supposed to enter first!"

Business focus refers to the ability to operate in a way that would help the business to prosper. It is all about making the right decision that works the best for the organisation. The Manager has to make sure that the organisation's main objective percolates well down the different layers of hierarchy and reaches the individuals of the company. Then he has to make sure that his activities are aligned with those of the organisation.

With this competency:
One understands the structure, strategy and overall goals of an organisation and aligns own activity with these; understands how own role links to other areas and the implications of actions for other parts of the business; recognises and uses the organisation's decision-making processes.

LEVELS OF PROFICIENCY
Proficiency Level C

"From next month, this is the new look for our front office ladies!"

- Uses own knowledge of the whole organisation to define possible new business.
- Creates a vision and strategic objectives for others to work towards.
- Identifies future goals and leads groups to reach them.
- Brings cultural changes into the company necessary for business situation.

> "Concentration can be cultivated. One can learn to exercise willpower, discipline one's body and train one's mind."
> – *Anil Ambani*
>
> "You've got a job to do, and because you've got a job to do, you've got to focus on that, so you don't have time for personal considerations."
> – *Dick Cheney*

Proficiency Level B

*"I am not firing you. I can't afford it!
I am asking you to resign due to personal problems!"*

- Takes impact on organisation into account when dealing with problems.
- Thinks through the implications for other parts of the business, aligns own plans/activities and decision making.
- Aware of politics of situation (sensitivities both internal and external).
- Sees the big picture and makes the links; has broad perspective.
- Understands issues across the business and initiates strategic discussions.
- Aware of top management thinking, and vision e.g., technical and non-technical aspects.

"Along with a strong belief in your own inner voice, you also need laserlike focus combined with unwavering determination."
  – Larry Flynt

"My success, part of it certainly, is that I have focused in on a few things."
  – Bill Gates

"A corporation is a living organism; it has to continue to shed its skin. Methods have to change. Focus has to change. Values have to change. The sum total of those changes is transformation."
  – Andrew Grove

Proficiency Level A

"Sir, I am confident we will close this deal for the land. The villagers are thrilled seeing our film on what this place will be after 10 years!"

- Focuses on objectives of the company.
- Understands organisation's power structure.
- Has in-depth understanding of business processes and approaches.
- Identifies and uses key stakeholders, internal and external.
- Understands the distribution chain.

"We wanted Nike to be the world's best sports and fitness company. Once you say that, you have a focus. You don't end up making wing tips or sponsoring the next Rolling Stones world tour."

– Philip Knight

"Next in importance to having a good aim is to recognise when to pull the trigger."

– David Letterman

"I was at the end of my tether when my first book was published. For eight years I didn't make a penny, I worked so hard, didn't drink, didn't enjoy life."

– Orhan Pamuk

Case Studies

From the World of Business

1. Ford Motor Company – Jacques Nasser*

On 1st January 1999, Jacques Nasser was named the President and CEO of Ford Motor Company. He had strong business acumen and foresight and he wanted to make Ford Motor Co., an automotive consumer powerhouse, which would provide everything from credit to automotive repair and used parts.

Nasser used his decision-making power and uncanny sense of business opportunity to ensure the company's success. He brought in new people, new philosophies and new technologies and aimed at outdoing General Motors as the largest auto company in the world. He built a dynamic team of top executives and crafted a simple but powerful business mission for Ford Motor Co. In 1999, *Automotive News* voted Nasser the *Industry Leader of the Year*.

To increase profits, Nasser disposed off Ford's low-margin parts operation, Visteon Automotive Systems. He planned a cradle-to-grave strategy in which Ford would have a hand in everything from auto repair to junkyard recycling.

In March 1999, soon after becoming the CEO, he acquired Volvo for over 6 billion dollars. With Volvo, Nasser managed to strengthen Ford's presence in European-style luxury cars. He initiated efforts to overhaul the way Ford designed its cars and launched plans to increase the company's luxury-car sales. In the same month, Nasser created Premier Automotive Group (PAG) and moved Ford's luxury brands to it. The strategy was to prevent the luxury models such as Jaguar, Land Rover and Aston Martin from being diluted by Ford's more mainstream brands.

As part of his cradle-to-grave strategy, he diversified into adjacent segments of the car market place by acquiring Land Rover, manufacturer of Sports Utility Vehicles (SUVs). He also sought to expand Ford's role in automotive services, by buying Kwik-Fit, the British car repair business.

---

* Adapted from ICMR cases/caselets; the original versions can be procured from ICMR/accessed on the ICMR website.

He launched a series of Internet initiatives to connect more directly with consumers. He wanted to increase the availability of information to offer enormous benefits directly to the customers. Ford's e-commerce venture centered on Covisint, the world's largest online exchange, extending to the entire supplier-to-dealer automotive value chain. All those who interacted with Ford – the vendors, customers or employees, all had the option of dealing online. This brought immense customer feedback and satisfaction and impacted business positively.

The Learning

Level-C:
- Creates a vision and strategic objectives for others to work towards it.
- Uses own knowledge of the whole organisation to define possible new business.

Level-B:
- Sees the big picture and makes the links; has a broad perspective.

Level-A:
- Has in-depth understanding of business processes and approaches.

Other themes covered: Leadership, Business Focus

2. Humayun Dhanrajgir: Power of Persuasion*

Humayan Dhanrajgir retired as managing director of Kodak India Ltd., after spending most of his career at Glaxo. Humayun exudes a charming personality and confidence. He moved from an engineering background to marketing. At Glaxo, Humayun demonstrated a successful new launch model with 'Zinetac' wherein the actual launch was preceded by a medical symposia where world-renowned doctors

---

* Reproduced with permission, ©McGraw Hill Education, India, B4, Sector 63, Dist. Gautam Budh Nagar, Noida, U.P. 201301.

participated. This model was used to change Glaxo's image from a vitamin maker to a serious seller of prescription drugs.

After he joined Kodak, five years of exceptional growth followed, in which Humayun concentrated on expanding the business of Kodak. The first challenge he successfully handled was that of selling India to Eastman Kodak. The turnover shot up from around Rs 200 crore to nearly Rs 600 crore. He took many other measures and brought about a turnaround.

Humayun loved the challenge of achieving stretched targets and always worked to help Kodak scale unprecedented heights. This desire manifested itself once again when he first thought of starting a Kodak unit in Nepal. He saw that as a very significant dimension, for changing the company's wealth-creation strategy. He analysed that they were too dependent on input, with low margins and falling prices (because the Japanese Yen was falling). Moreover, local distributors were playing tricks with customers, evading sales tax and so forth.

Humayun needed a strategic weapon to combat this situation. He began to study all possible alternatives. He knew that Nepal was keen to industrialise. If Kodak set up a unit in Nepal, an added benefit would be that they could bring these films into India without paying duty because of trade agreements with the Himalayan kingdom. Humayun's persuasion and foresight paid off once again; the approval took 8-10 months but the Nepal unit became a 100 per cent subsidiary of Kodak India.

The key was Humayun's transparent dealings and sincere efforts that impressed the Nepali bureaucrats. There were no bribes nor any middlemen, only factual information and expert knowledge and managerial skills.

The Learning

Level-C:
- Identifies future goals and leads groups to reach them.

Level-B:
- Understands issues across the business and initiates strategic discussions and implementation.

Other themes covered: Leadership, Communication.

2. Dhirubhai Ambani: Self-made Business Icon

There are scores of rags-to-riches stories one reads about, but there is only one Dhirubhai Ambani. He rose from working at a petrol pump, to set up the largest grassroots oil refinery in the world. He had to borrow Rs 100 to buy clothes for a job but ended up setting up the most modern textile mill in the country. He rose from being the one who waited for payment of paltry bills outside the cabins of purchase officers in mills, to become the greatest industrialist in the country. He finally made it to *Forbe's* list of the richest men in the world.

Even while working as an attendant in a Shell gas station, Dhirubhai was determined that he would one day head a company like Shell and go into oil business. Sceptics laughed, but he made his dream come true within one lifetime. In 1986, he declared that Reliance would in ten years be a Rs 80 billion company. Sales in 1995 rose to Rs 78 billion. The detractors were silenced – it was a testimonial to the man with extraordinary business acumen and vision.

The year 1958 witnessed his return to Mumbai where he started trading in spices such as ginger and turmeric. A firm, Reliance Commercial Cooperation, was simultaneously floated with capital of Rs 15,000. In 1959, Dhirubhai switched his trading business from spices to yarn in an office barely having table space in the Masjid Bunder area of Mumbai. There was no staff, only Dhirubhai himself and one Manubhai Sheth, who continues to be a part of the Ambani group even today.

Dhirubhai made a good profit in the yarn business and graduated from a yarn trader to a mill owner in 1966 by setting up a small textile mill at Naroda, near Ahmedabad. When he purchased a big chunk of barren land at a far away place for a small textile unit, he was ridiculed by many.

Later however, Dhirubhai was applauded for his great foresight and vision, when he expanded that small textile unit into India's most modern textile mill. This was a period when the Indian government allowed earnings from rayon fabric exports to be used for importing nylon fabrics. Moreover, the Indian government faced a massive foreign exchange crisis. Dhirubhai was able to see and seize the opportunity. He moved into exports in a big way. The massive profits made from exports to Russia, Poland, Zambia, Uganda, Saudi Arabia, etc., were used for expansion and modernisation of the Naroda mill.

In the year 1977, not getting a response from banks, Dhirubhai resorted to the only sure source of money – the public. Dhirubhai realised that in order to attract the public into investing in his schemes, he had to offer them something above and beyond what they were already used to getting. And this was the steady appreciation of their shareholding. He propounded it more than dividends; it was the capital appreciation that made the shareholders rich.

In 1989, another major resource generation step was taken, when Reliance Petrochemicals floated a Rs 516-crore public issue. Over 20 lakh investors responded. The year 1993 was another landmark for Reliance India Limited, when it emerged as India's largest private sector company with sales crossing the Rs 4000-crore mark. It also figured among the top 50 companies of the developing countries listed by *Business Week*.

Dhirubhai was a man with an earthy vocabulary, possessing no airs of a management genius or a great business tycoon. He attributed his success to being a step ahead of the main competition, looking ahead and getting results with most of the bold steps and decisions that he took.

The Learning

Level-C:
- Identifies future goals and leads groups to reach them.

Level-B:
- Understands issues across the business and initiates strategic discussions and implementation.

Level-A:
- Identifies and uses key stakeholders.

Other themes covered: Leadership, Decision making, Personal Responsibility.

Achieving Business Results

2. Cost & Profit Management

"We have installed a new security system with which we can have just one guard per shift!"

The profitability of many companies in mature markets and industries is increasingly under threat due to various competitive factors. Competitors are passing cost savings (gained through moving supply bases and entire functions to lower-cost environments) through to customers thereby depressing prices; top line revenue growth is stagnant as customers have a wider choice and become more demanding in what they buy and at which price; increasing levels of product/service substitution are driving the continuous need to understand market and its impact on operations strategy and profitability; and customers are restricting their spending in uncertain economic and political times. Likewise, companies in emerging growth markets and industries are faced with the challenge of nurturing the growth of their revenue line without eroding their profitability by aggressively expanding their cost base.

With this Competency:
One considers issues in terms of cost and profit; seeks to maximize return on activity; and understands commercial and financial principles.

LEVELS OF PROFICIENCY

Proficiency Level C

"If our production comes down, sir, due to the new technology, we can push this as a CDM project and earn money!"

- Develops strategic indicators for the future of own area.
- Anticipates and develops a long-term plan for achievement of objectives.
- Determines the necessary qualitative and quantitative resources in order to achieve efficiency.

> "A man must be big enough to admit his mistakes, smart enough to profit from them, and strong enough to correct them."
> – *John C. Maxwell*
>
> "Make every thought, every fact, that comes into your mind pay you a profit. Make it work and produce for you. Think of things not as they are but as they might be. Don't merely dream – but create!"
> – *Robert Collier*

Proficiency Level B

"I did say half is better than one-third, but I didn't ask you to knock off the driver before our escape!"

- Analyses risks and evaluates implications of activities for medium- to long-term profit.
- Analyses and interprets data in order to identify ways to maintain profit in the medium term.
- Identifies and proposes new approaches, outside own area as well, to reduce costs.

"If you don't do it excellently, don't do it at all. Because if it's not excellent, it won't be profitable or fun, and if you're not in business for fun or profit, what the hell are you doing there?"
— *Robert Townsend*

"The more you say, the less people remember. The fewer the words, the greater the profit."
— *Unknown*

"The investor of today does not profit from yesterday's growth."
— *Warren Buffett*

Proficiency Level A

"As the company grows, so will you. But I cannot give you a raise right now. Our motto is 'save a rupee, earn a rupee'!"

- Understands commercial and financial principles e.g., P/L and margin.
- Is aware of impact of own function/area on costs and uses people and time effectively.
- Identifies possible alternative solutions for the one to improve efficiency and profit.
- Considers the financial implications of action e.g., negotiating.
- Pragmatically identifies the most effective and efficient ways to employ people and time.

"Remind people that profit is the difference between revenue and expense. This makes you look smart."
— *Scott Adams*

"Profits, like sausages... are esteemed most by those who know least about what goes into them."
— *Alvin Toffler*

"If you mean to profit, learn to please."
— *Winston Churchill*

"To get profit without risk, experience without danger, and reward without work, is as impossible as it is to live without being born."
— *A. P. Gouthev*

Case Studies

From the World of Business

1. Telco Turnaround – Bold and Persistent

Chairman of Tata Engineering and Locomotive Company, Ratan Tata led a major turnaround for Telco in 2002.

The truckmaker (renamed Tata Motors in July 2003) survived one of its biggest crises ever, after it pumped in over Rs 1,700 crore for the dream of being a car maker. Even well-wishers and insiders worried about the decision to launch a debut car to compete with the world's best in a 50-model crowded industry.

The investment in the car project came at a time when its core business of commercial vehicles was struggling due to a sluggish economy, low demand and increased competition. After news of the ambitious venture hit markets, the company's share price collapsed by over 50 per cent in one year to hit an all-time low of Rs 58 in May 2001. Everyone was just waiting for the giant to fall. But the Tatas just did not give up.

For the financial year ended 31st March 2003, Telco posted a consolidated net profit of Rs 298.67 crore, compared to a net loss of Rs 107.19 crore in 2002. The loss was about Rs 500 crore in 2001.

In May 2003, the company sales grew 21 per cent to Rs 9,093 crore for the entire year as it sold 219,859 vehicles. And its share price bounced back to the Rs 165-175 band.

While its car business received the consumer's full attention, Telco's commercial vehicle sales also topped the sales growth chart with a 30 per cent growth in FY 2003 to 1.07 lakh – the highest in over five years.

The main reason for Telco's turnaround has been the speedy 'mid-way correction' by Bombay House (Tata's South Mumbai headquarters), after consumers rejected the first lot of Indicas. The bad press followed soon after. And then Version 2 was launched after modification based on careful analysis of user feedback. The turnaround came as a result of various measures including cost saving, restructuring, volume rise and aggressive marketing.

Apart from product modification, the Ratan Tata, Chairman, Telco personally roped in Dr V. Sumantran from General Motors of United States to give more focus to the company's passenger car business.

The car was also made more affordable. Barring the first lot of dissatisfied customers, the company's Indica V2 – selling at around Rs 3.55 lakhs in Thane – was the cheapest diesel car to own. Its running costs were low and, of course, it was the real Made-in-India car.

"It did well due to its fuel efficiency. Its nearest competitor was priced Rs 30,000 more. It was a big cost advantage for the price-sensitive Indian customer."

Ratan Tata blamed the bad days on the general economic recession and not so much on company strategy. He pointed out that Tata Group would have to build a presence in overseas markets, particularly for Tata Motors, Indian Hotels and TCS through joint ventures or a new enterprise. And that is the path the Tatas have taken since 2004.

The Learning

Level-C:
- Anticipates and develops a long-term plan for achievements of objective.

Level-B:
- Analyses risks and evaluates implications of activities for medium- to long-term profit.

Level-A:
- Considers financial implications of action e.g., negotiating.

Other themes covered: Leadership, Business Focus.

2. Nissan Turnaround Story*

Carlos Ghosn is a big name in the industry. He led the most dramatic turnaround of an automaker's fortunes in recent times. He is today known as the turnaround specialist. One of the stiffest challenges he faced was bringing back Nissan from the brink.

In a period (the late nineties) when most automakers were struggling to make a profit (in spite of strong sales), Nissan Motor Company reported its best financial results in history – $2.7 billion in net profit for fiscal year 2000, ended March 31, 2001. Results for the first half of the 2001 fiscal year included a 34 per cent improvement in net income over the same period a year ago and a robust operating margin of 6.3 per cent. This followed after a decade of dismal performance and surprised most experts.

To understand the true scope of this revival, consider that the company, once a leader in its home market – building a third of all the cars sold in Japan – had contracted by 1999 to a market share slightly over half that size. Nissan North America Inc., meanwhile, one of the earliest Japanese automaker's jump into the U.S. market, was the one that stumbled most visibly.

Like Toyota, Nissan had established a footprint with small, reliable pickup trucks at the end of the 1950s. Then it followed with the Datsun 240Z.

Nissan lost track by bringing out unimaginative products conceived by Japanese engineers blind to American tastes. It made a slow entry into important market segments like minivans and SUVs. Despite repeated efforts of top executives, Nissan lost market share worldwide for 10 years, and failed to generate profits for most of the 1980s.

The dramatic turn came in March 1999, when automaker Renault signed an agreement to take a controlling interest in Nissan of 37 per cent and installed Ghosn, then an executive vice president at the French company, as COO. The Renault/Nissan Alliance, brought Ghosn and a 200-member French management team to Japan to map out Nissan's future.

---

* Adapted from ICMR cases/caselets; the original versions can be procured from ICMR/accessed on the ICMR website.

The blueprint Ghosn and his team drafted, became known as the Nissan Revival Plan, which was released in October 1999. The strategy came right out of the turnaround specialist's playbook: cut costs (by lowering worldwide headcount by 21,000, closing five plants in Japan and reducing purchasing outlays by 20 per cent); slash debt; and divest assets. Less evident was the plan's ownership provision that Ghosn enforced in order to ensure its embrace. "From the beginning, it was clear the plan would be a Nissan plan; we didn't hire any consultants and Renault executives served only as facilitators and coaches," says Ghosn. "The plan would be built by Nissan people and every team, every department, every employee [would know] what his or her own contribution would be."

It wasn't just the mid-level managers who faced the risks ahead. To emphasise the urgency of a do-or-die commitment, Ghosn's team agreed to a pact of their own: "We said very clearly that if any one of the goals were not reached, the president of the company and executive committee would resign."

When Renault took its stake in Nissan, industry observers predicted a collision of cultures, particularly because the French automaker did not operate on anything like the global scale of its new partner. Nissan's dire need for a saviour may have helped smooth the process. At the same time, Ghosn's own multicultural background helped to bring a broader perspective to the relationship.

To ensure that the Japanese engineers understood their French managers, Ghosn designated English as the common language. But still the company had to overcome the potential for varying definitions of important concepts. To solve the problem a team created a dictionary of essential terms. When Ghosn noticed that some key words were not understood the same way by different Japanese people or even different French people, he established a dictionary for the 100 key words in management, with clear definitions.

Nissan's resurrection is all the more remarkable because it is a structural reworking of business practices; notable turnarounds by competitors have been product driven.

Chrysler, for example, found success through inventing the contemporary minivan and Volkswagen reaped renewed public affection, thanks to the much-adored profile of the New Beetle.

Nissan has stayed the course set out under the Nissan Revival Plan and has thrown its energy into meeting its original business objectives, which concentrate on fundamentals rather than a sudden flood of new models. Ghosn brought to the scene a clear focus of priorities and a clear plan by which to execute those priorities. He did not waver from the start to the finish.

When Ghosn and his team began to assess Nissan's desperate situation, there was no shortage of advice. People warned, "against touching the keiretsu system," Japan's system of interlocking industrial cartels. "You can't close plants in Japan, you can't reduce headcount in Japan," many said.

Ghosn admits that he had to choose between accepting outside advice and doing something that would be inadequate to get the company out of trouble or forgetting what he heard and going for what was necessary for the company to change. He said, "It was uncharted territory. I finally considered that if I was chief operating officer, my one option was to fix the problems not to try to water them down."

The Learning

Level-C:
- Anticipates and develops a long-term plan for achievements of objective.

Level-B:
- Identifies and proposes new approaches, outside own area as well, to reduce costs.

Level-A:
- Pragmatically identifies the most effective and efficient ways to employ people and time.

Other themes covered: Communication, Leadership.

3. Gillette's Restructuring in India*

Gillette India Limited (GIL), the Indian arm of The Gillette Company (Gillette), the world's largest manufacturer of shaving products, had been in India for a decade and a half by 1998-99 but was unable to generate the expected growth. In particular, the company's net profit margin took a severe beating during the period 1998-2000. To turn around the company, in 1999-2000 GIL started a restructuring programme – a three-pronged programme. It focused on functional excellence, a strategic re-look at the organisation and a financial turnaround. The firm implemented the first with the objective of benchmarking and improving systems, processes and resource deployment in the company with that of the industry as a whole.

This resulted in increased productivity, lower overheads and working capital deployment. At the strategic level, the company exited from non-profitable and non-strategic businesses to focus on profitable businesses. It concentrated on the grooming and oral care business and exited the battery and household appliances activities.

For the financial turnaround, the company paid attention to working capital management and improvement in operating efficiencies. The company achieved a 56 per cent reduction in net working capital from Rs 1.56 billion to Rs 684.2 million between December 2001 and December 2002. There was decrease in receivables, product lines and inventories. The savings were put into marketing. Improved performances in key product segments and effective cost management resulted in GIL achieving a turnaround in the early 2000s.

Gillette India realised that it had to focus on the dominant double-edge segment to hike topline growth for its male grooming business. The company entered 2003 with strong fundamentals, focused goals of profitable sales growth and consolidation of last year's gains.

Gillette India (formerly Indian Shaving Products Ltd.) is a subsidiary of the Gillette Company, and after its merger

---

* Adapted from ICMR cases/caselets; the original versions can be procured from ICMR/accessed on the ICMR website.

with Wilkinson Sword India Ltd., and Duracell India Ltd., it expanded its portfolio to include the core shaving products business across price-points, batteries and oral care.

The company closed 2002 with a net profit of Rs 6.46 crore against a net loss of Rs 27.79 crore the previous year. While grooming sales declined by 1.7 per cent, diversified operations comprising oral care, personal care and household products increased 16.4 per cent. SensorExcel grew by 16.4 per cent while Mach 3 grew by 54.2 per cent by volumes. The portable power division emerged as the leader in the alkaline battery market with a 56 per cent share. The company's key strategic decisions included exiting non-performing categories, reducing non-strategic promotions, rationalisation of product lines, manufacturing efficiencies, reduction in overheads and going aggressive in the mass blades segment.

In 2001, when Gillette sold its Jeep battery business to the Thanawalla group, it was affirmed that the focus was on building the Duracell alkaline battery business. Maintaining production of zinc batteries in India did not support this direction.

Gillette in 2002 went through a significant strategic turnaround. Manoj Kumar, Regional Business Director, (Grooming & Personal Care), India and South Asia, Gillette India explained this as, "The topline for our grooming business needs to grow faster. The company which has so far been creating and promoting high-end systems and disposables, will focus on the high-volume, double-edge segment."

A market study had shown a dominant 97 per cent of the Rs 600 crore blades' market comprises the double-edge segment, about half of which is accounted for by salon usage. Systems and disposables account for just about 3 per cent of this market.

Gillette India couldn't have ignored the double-edge segment for long as the volume was there. By the end of 2001, the 7 O' clock brand was re-positioned and re-branded as Gillette 7 O' clock. An aggressive marketing plan had the company breaking a new television campaign. Set against the theme of a 'platinum girl' concept, it attempted to drive home the platinum edge attribute which comes coated on the 7 O'clock blade.

This benefit needed to be effectively communicated to the consumers. The advertising campaign was educative yet not pedantic and was taken forward through on-ground activities across the year. Gillette was not going to go mass all out. The focus was on the large double-edge segment but brands such as Mach 3 and the Series range remained very much at the premium end.

The Learning

Level-C:
- Determines the necessary qualitative and quantitative resources in order to achieve efficiency.

Level-B:
- Identifies and proposes new approaches, outside own area as well, to reduce costs.

Level-A:
- Identifies possible alternative solutions for the one to improve efficiency and profit.

Other themes covered: Business Focus, Planning and Organising.

Achieving Business Results

3. Service Focus

"Now that's what I call service, everything together in one go!"

This seems obvious in the context of business to require much elucidation. Yet it is not so simple unless it is a service-oriented industry like hospitality, airlines, etc., where the customer is clearly visible. In every case it is important to *give a voice to the customer* and find a way to align the organisation's business goals with the needs and desires of the customer. This may often imply hard decisions like accepting thinner margins of profit and investing heavily in capturing the attention of the potential customer through advertising and marketing strategies which do not always succeed in a highly competitive environment.

With this competency:

One focuses on the needs of customers e.g., end-customers, dealers and internal customers; understands situations from the customer's perspective and provides solutions, which fit with customer's needs; and even puts customer requirements before own needs.

LEVELS OF PROFICIENCY

Proficiency Level C

"Excuse me Sir! May I request you to fill up this customer feedback form?"

- Establishes a professional relationship with key influencers in the client organisations.
- Monitors continuously client satisfaction. Partners with the client over the long term.
- Ensures that all services provided to clients reflect a consistently high level of quality.

> "... the real focus should be on people who are buying today because the Companies are starting to measure how effective their customer service is and trying to understand what they can do to improve the customer service process."
> – *Sanjay Kumar*
>
> "Be dramatically willing to focus on the customer at all costs, even at the cost of obsoleting your own stuff."
> – *Scott Cook*

Proficiency Level B

"Please step in! We are not quite closed yet, Sir!"

- Sets up systems/procedures to ensure ongoing feedback from customers in order to anticipate problems and to address future needs.
- Considers a situation from customers perspective.
- Keeps abreast of service levels of suppliers and costs associated.
- Is sensitive to customer satisfaction.

"Firms need to ensure that their ability to provide effective customer service keeps pace with their growth. If you're marketing your firm to new customers, you better be able to provide them service when they do business with you."
— *Arthur Levitt*

"A merchant who approaches business with the idea of serving the public well has nothing to fear from the competition."
— *JamesCash Penney*

Proficiency Level A

"It's all right ma'am. He is such a sweet playful child!"

- Focuses on customer needs and feelings.
- Seeks to understand and resolve customer problems in a timely fashion, e.g., asks questions/resources, keeps informed, takes ownership.
- Presents professional image, e.g., displays emotional control, is polite and respectful with difficult customers.
- Treats customer individually and with empathy and patience.
- Puts customer needs before own personal needs.
- Treats internal customers as external customers.

"A store's best advertisement is the service its goods render, for upon such service rests the future, the goodwill, of an organisation."
– *James Cash Penney*

"Wal-Mart's internal customer service standards reminded me of the philosophy of the Three Musketeers – 'It's all for one and one for all!'"
– *Michael Bergdahl*

"He profits most who serves best."
– *Arthur F. Sheldon*

Case Studies

From the World of Business

1. Bharat Petroleum Corporation Ltd., (BPCL)*

The petrol pump in India was not an exciting place to be in hardly a decade ago. With the deregulation of the oil industry, a need to be more customer focused was felt by the Indian oil majors. From thereon, petrol pumps in India have come a long way from being dusty, poorly-lit places manned by shabbily-clothed personnel, to the shopping malls of today. Bharat Petroleum Corporation Ltd., (BPCL), a leading player in the Indian petroleum industry, pioneered vast changes in the Indian fuel retailing business.

BPCL's first foray into petrol pump retailing was through Bharat Shell Ltd., (SHELL) its joint venture with Shell Overseas Investments of Netherlands. Shell launched the first convenience store (C-Store) stocking over a 1000 different items. The store, offering eatables, soft drinks, stationery, newspapers, magazines, frozen foods, light bulbs, audiocassettes and CDs, came as a pleasant surprise for Indian consumers used to garage-like settings.

In October 2000, BPCL pioneered another revolutionary concept by launching a McDonald's fast food outlet at a petrol pump near Mathura (UP) on the Delhi-Agra Highway.

BPCL closely studied the consumer behaviour and found that most customers arrived between 8 p.m. to 11 p.m. So the company decided to keep the stores open till at least 11 p.m., making a positive impact on sales.

To offer enhanced services to its customers, BPCL tied up with various companies from a number of different industries: fast food, photography, music, financial services, ISPs, greeting cards, ATMs, e-commerce portals and courier services. The companies involved were McDonald's, Tata Internet Service Ltd., Pepsi, Kwality Walls, DHL, Sony,

---

* Adapted from ICMR cases/caselets; the original versions can be procured from ICMR/accessed on the ICMR website.

Service Focus 141

Canon, ITC, UTI Bank, etc. These companies were all given counters within the stores for selling their products and services.

BPCL had shown the path for other players to follow. Soon, BPCL's rivals, IOC and HPCL, also began refurbishing their petrol pumps. The one who gained the most from this newfound retail focus of the oil companies, was the customer.

The Learning

Level-C:
- Monitors client satisfaction continuously.

Level-B:
- Considers situation from customers perspective.

Other themes covered: Business Focus, Managing Change.

2. Jack Welch and GE – Meeting Customer Demands

Jack Welch always viewed GE as a company to be driven by customers. He recognised that it was vital to understand the customer's particular quality demands. Keeping this in mind, Jack Welch initiated the Six Sigma program. Customer satisfaction and loyalty were vital elements of the Six Sigma program at GE at all levels. In the mid 1990s, Six Sigma program had a big role to play in the company.

Six Sigma was originally intended to serve as a quality control benchmark for manufacturing. Jack Welch transformed this to focus on virtually all service-related transactions. GE learned and developed the complex Six Sigma program through internal and external benchmarking research. Though the methodologies of six Sigma were learned from other companies, but the all-encompassing passion for it was pure GE.

Jack attributed three factors to the success of Six Sigma program at GE: aligning employee benefits and promotions with Six sigma programs; demanding a high degree of senior management support to define objectives and facilitate implementation; and working to demonstrate the impact of the Six Sigma initiatives to customers.

The employees engaged in the Six Sigma discipline were categorised as Green Belt and Black Belt champions. No employee was considered for a management position unless they had some Green Belt training and completed at least one Six Sigma program. GE took a top-down approach to ensure that the best employees became Black Belts. Jack Welch personally supervised the progress that business units made in their Six Sigma programs. Furthermore, Black Belts and Master Black Belts add a high degree of visibility to the company's senior management team and were responsible for mentoring and coaching Green Belts. GE reinforced the importance of the Six Sigma program by linking it with managerial compensation. About 40 per cent of each GE executive's bonus was linked to Six Sigma implementation, which applied to the top 7000 executives.

Jack Welch was the primary driver of the Six Sigma program at GE. He constantly defined and adjusted the specific objectives for the program. He spoke frequently to the organisation regarding the program's development and continually emphasised its value during conferences/meetings and through publications such as annual reports. Almost every GE division leader combined the Six Sigma methodology with company culture and goals. Each division implemented Six Sigma with project teams, overseen by senior management.

Thus, Jack Welch turned the Six Sigma company vision 'outside in' to make 'the customer's profitability the number one priority in any process improvement.' In 1998, GE Capital generated over U.S.$300,000 million as net income from Six Sigma improvements. The Six Sigma program increased the company's operating profit margins from 13.6 per cent in 1995 to 16.7 per cent in the third quarter of 1999.

> **The Learning**
>
> *Level-C:*
> - Partners with the client over the long term.
>
> *Level-B:*
> - Treats internal customers as external customers.
>
> *Level-A:*
> - Focuses on customer needs and feelings.

Other themes covered: Business Focus.

2. Deepak Parekh & HDFC's Customer Focus*

When Deepak Parekh joined HDFC in 1979, an entrepreneur par excellence was destined to be born. In a little over two decades, under Parekh's leadership, the Housing Development Finance Corporation (HDFC) had become a model financial institution. It had grown at an average of 78 per cent in the late nineties. Deepak Parekh became synonymous with this outstanding professional institution which has housed millions of people across the country.

HDFC became a brand because of its spectacular track record of creating and expanding India's home mortgage market earning the gratitude of over one million middle class homeowners. It has become a financial supermarket, offering a range of services from banking (HDFC Bank) and consumer finance (Countrywide) to infrastructure finance and leasing (IDFC and ILRFS) and more lately, insurance.

In about two decades, Parekh translated a social need into a highly profitable business with consistent returns. Spotting the business opportunity in the housing needs of urban India and exploiting this, was an act of supreme entrepreneurship. Parekh focused on the middle classes before anybody else and won their loyalty by providing what they needed, from housing to banking services, and from consumer finance to infrastructure development facilities.

---

* Reproduced with permission, ©McGraw Hill Education, India, B4, Sector 63, Dist. Gautam Budh Nagar, Noida, U.P. 201301.

Parekh's action agenda for change[1] put the customer centre-stage by:
- Focusing on customer service rather than eligibility criteria;
- Developing customer-friendly procedures;
- Suiting repayment methods to customer requirements;
- Simplifying the loan process – cutting down paperwork to a bare minimum, speeding up approvals, and computerising transactions.
- All this also meant reducing the number of times the customer needed to visit HDFC offices.

Efforts were made to change attitudes of the staff so that the focus would be customer convenience instead of a loan target. Front office was designed in such a manner that the customer could feel comfortable and discuss his loan privately. Why was all this so important at HDFC? "We offer three very clear reasons: *Own the information, set the standards, and keep the customers,*" recalls Parekh.

About Parekh's vision, Keshub Mahindra, vice chairman of HDFC and chairman of the Mahindra & Mahindra group, once said, "His ability to see the big picture before anybody else, and then to systematically focus on each of its components, is as unique as it is remarkable."[2]

HDFC was involved in asset management and insurance, two huge areas. To quote Parekh, "We are the last to enter in asset management. How do we mobilise money when 22 organisations are there? It's a question of relationship. So one should be competent in building relationships."

Parekh knows that building relationships is a core competency. Trust and faith are of prime importance for creating opportunities. In the first 10 to 15 years, people came to HDFC for loans. Their deposit schemes failed to gather momentum and mop up savings. It took effort and time to

---

[1] *Thought Leaders: The Source Code of Exceptional Managers and Entrepreneurs* by Shrinivas Pandit. Tata McGraw-Hill Publishing Company Limited, New Delhi, 2002 (reprint) p.255.
[2] Ibid. p.257.

build trust. After a few years, people started trusting the company as a recognised saving institution, rather than as a lending one. With over 12 lakh depositors (many of them are public charitable trusts) and eight lakh borrowers, trust, safety and security have got institutionalised and become equated with the HDFC name.

What drives Parekh? He says, "The satisfaction of making people happy." Parekh recalls an episode over twenty years ago when Narayana Murthy, the Infosys chairman, took a loan of Rs 70,000 for a small flat. His wife was standing there and praying. He didn't know anybody, but without paying a bribe or using influence he got the money.[3] Today Narayana Murthy could buy HDFC. But he will remember his experience with us. One's home is the single biggest asset purchased by any human being in his lifetime. The happiness, the thrill, the satisfaction – it's magnificent."

Parekh acted like an entrepreneur. He masterminded every scheme and made his colleagues do the same. He gave them freedom and process ownership, without interfering, and they gave him the results. As he says, "We at HDFC are not just managers, but entrepreneurs and leaders as well." Parekh foresees the need for a new breed of leaders? He says, "Predicting the future will be much more important in a period of rapid change than it has been hitherto, and our skills for this are sadly lacking. Defining core competency will be more important than ever before. Competitive forces will ensure that we stick to what we know best".

Parekh says, "Tomorrow's leaders will need newer skill sets; they will need to be far more aware of international trends and global information. They will also need to be aware that as tariff barriers around the world are increasingly rationalised, their corporations must be capable of sustaining such changes to effectively compete even in domestic markets."[4] Good leadership results in sustainable brand equity. *In the long term, integrity, transparency, quality and*

---

[3] Thought Leaders... op. cit. p.269
[4] Ibid. p.271.

higher levels of service do more for the brand than any advertising or communication program. Leadership involves many concepts. For Parekh, it speaks of a team of committed managers, cohesively working towards corporate excellence.

The Learning

Level-C:
- Partners with the client over the long term.

Level-B:
- Treats internal customers as external customers.

Level-A:
- Focuses on customer needs and feelings.

Other themes covered: Business Focus, Leadership.

Professional Improvement

1. Managing Changing Environment

"That is the new supervision team for the factory!"

Change is inevitable and normal – an essential aspect of human life, which creates new opportunities for growth and development, and challenges every individual to fulfill his or her potential. Change has always been the hallmark of successful organisations. Only the pace of change has quickened.

An important aspect of leadership is managing change. In order to harness the positive energy of change, a leader needs to keep an open mind and be receptive. Change is inevitable. The most holistic approach that he can make is to embrace it, work with it and ultimately make it work for the organisation. A leader needs to be very flexible so that when change occurs he can change gears comfortably. He should have the ability to adapt behaviour and work methods in response to the new information.

With this competency:

One is open to change, is flexible and adaptable to changing circumstances and tolerant of ambiguity and fluidity within the organisation e.g., lack of clear structure; is able to identify where change is necessary and is willing to take calculated risks to achieve it; enrolls support of others to achieve and manage change.

LEVELS OF PROFICIENCY
Proficiency Level C

"Don't worry! This setback has taught us so much!! Just keep up the good work!!"

- Evaluates impact of change on own organisational environment.
- Clarifies direction and priorities for others.
- Introduces new approaches and work methods for managing change.
- Promotes evaluation of risk and exploration of innovative pathways.
- Reassesses situations in light of changing priorities.
- Learns and builds on accomplishments and setbacks.

"Only the wisest and stupidest of men never change."
– *Confucius*

"One key to successful leadership is continuous personal change. Personal change is a reflection of our inner growth and empowerment."
– *Robert E. Quinn*

"Whosoever desires constant success must change his conduct with the times."
– *Niccolo Machiavelli*

"People don't resist change. They resist being changed!"
– *Peter Senge*

Proficiency Level B

"Bringing in women staff is a calculated risk. Output is likely to go up but may fall marginally later!"

- Tolerant of ambiguity and fluidity e.g., lack of clear structure and direction.
- Prepared to take calculated risks to achieve change.
- Adjusts to changing circumstances and new ways of working.
- Prepared to compromise on own view to accommodate wider business needs.
- Open to change and foster change.
- Applies understanding of the reason for change to develop new plans. Follows up on opportunities to make positive change.

> "Change is hard because people overestimate the value of what they have – and underestimate the value of what they may gain by giving that up."
> - *James Belasco and Ralph Stayer*
> Flight of the Buffalo (1994)

> "There is nothing more difficult to take in hand, more perilous to conduct, or more uncertain in its success, than to take the lead in the introduction of a new order of things."
> - *Niccolo Machiavelli*
> The Prince (1515)

> "The rate of change is not going to slow down anytime soon. If anything, competition in most industries will probably speed up even more in the next few decades."
> - *John P. Kotter*
> Leading Change

Proficiency Level A

"While the visitors are here please occupy my seat. It will have a greater impact!"

- Prepared to tackle unfamiliar areas.
- Prepared to handle tasks outside of own role.
- Takes a flexible approach and shifts focus as required.
- Adapts own behaviour to new requirements.
- Cooperates with changing plans and priorities.

> "There is a certain relief in change, even though it be from bad to worse; as I have found in traveling in a stagecoach, that it is often a comfort to shift one's position and be bruised in a new place."
> – **Washington Irving**
> Tales of a Traveler (1824)

> "We are chameleons, and our partialities and prejudices change place with an easy and blessed facility, and we are soon wonted to the change and happy in it."
> – **Mark Twain**

Case Studies

From the World of Business

1. K. V. Kamath: Change Management at ICICI

This is the story of change management at India's leading financial services company, ICICI after K. V. Kamath took over as its head following the ICICI Bank and Bank of Madura merger.

In May 1996, K. V. Kamath became the CEO of Industrial Credit and Investment Corporation of India (ICICI) after a stint with Asian Development Bank in Manila. Immediately after taking charge, Kamath introduced massive changes in the organisational structure. The changes undoubtedly brought in a lot of confusion and resentment among the employees. Let's see what these changes were and how effectively Kamath managed them.

Kamath realised that in the de-regulated environment, ICICI was neither a low-cost player nor was it a differentiator in terms of customer service. The change programme was initiated within the organisation, the first move being the creation of different departments – infrastructure, oil and gas, planning and treasury department, etc. Kamath picked up people from different departments who were considered to be good for these departments.

As most majority of the work and talent shifted to the corporate centre, employees at zonal offices felt their importance was diminishing. Another consequence of the department formation was that if a client had three different requirements from ICICI, he had to approach the relevant departments separately. The process was time consuming and there was a danger that the client would take a portion of that business elsewhere. To tackle this problem, ICICI set up three new departments: Major Client Group (MCG), Growth Client Group (GCG) and Personal Finance Group (PFG). Now the problem was that bigger clients in the MCG group required more diverse kinds of services. So employees in other departments felt that working in MCG offered better exposure and bigger orders.

Kamath was quick to deny this. He clarified that just being in MCG did not guarantee anything and these positions were to be rotated as required.

While Kamath's comments in the media seemed to discuss many of the employee complaints, ICICI was in fact, putting in place a host of measures to check this unrest. Training programmes and seminars were conducted for around 257 officers by external agencies, covering different areas. In addition, in-house training programmes were conducted in Pune and Mumbai. During 1995-96, 35 officers were nominated for overseas training programmes. ICICI also introduced a two-year Graduates' Management Training Programme (GMTP) for offices in the Junior Management Grades.

Apart from this, the management also took steps to set right the rewards system. Compensation policy was also restructured. Two types of remuneration were considered — type one was a contract basis to attract risk-takers and the second was tenure based which would appeal to employees who wanted security. Soon, a 360-degree appraisal system was put in place.

As a result of the above measures, the employee unrest gradually gave way to a much more relaxed atmosphere within the company.

Once again in December 2000, ICICI had to face change resistance when ICICI Bank was merged with Bank of Madura (BoM). Though ICICI Bank was nearly three times the size of BoM, its staff strength was only 1,400 as against BoM's 2,500. Half of BoM's personnel were clerks and around 350 were subordinate staff.

These were large differences in profiles, grades, designations and salaries of personnel in the two entities. It was also reported that there was uneasiness among the staff of BoM as they felt that ICICI would push up the productivity per employee, to match the levels of ICICI. BoM employees feared that their positions would come in for closer scrutiny.

The apprehensions of the BoM employee seemed to be justified as the working cultures at ICICI and BoM were quite different.

ICICI not only put in place several measures to technologically upgrade the BoM branches to ICICI's standards, but also paid special attention to facilitate a smooth cultural integration. The company appointed consultants Hewitt Associates to help in working out a uniform compensation and work culture and to take care of any change management problems. ICICI conducted an employee behavioural-pattern study to assess the various fears and sense of alienation employees typically went through during a merger.

Based on the study findings, ICICI established systems to take care of the employee resistance with actions rather than words.

To ensure employee participation and to decrease the resistance to the change, management established clear communication channels throughout to neutralise any kind of wrong messages being sent across. Training programmes were conducted which emphasised on knowledge, skill, attitude and technology to upgrade skills of the employees. Management also worked on contingency plans and initiated direct dialogue with the employee unions of the BoM to maintain good employee relations.

By June 2001, the process of integration between ICICI and BoM was started. ICICI transferred around 450 BoM employees to ICICI bank, while 300 ICICI employees were shifted to BoM branches. Promotion schemes for BoM employees were initiated and around 800 BoM officers were found to be eligible for promotions. By the end of the year, ICICI seemed to have successfully handled the HR aspects of the BoM merger. The scenario created by HR initiatives resulted in high level of morale among all sections of the employees from the erstwhile BoM.

In 2001 *CNBC* named Kamath 'Asian Business Leader of the Year' and *Business India* named him 'Businessman of the Year' in 2005.

> **The Learning**
>
> *Level-C:*
> - Clarifies direction and priorities for others.
>
> *Level-B:*
> - Prepared to take calculated risks to achieve change.

Other themes covered: Leadership, Communication.

2. Jagdish Khattar: Re-packaging Maruti

When the Indian car industry opened its doors to new players, Maruti Udyog Ltd., (MUL) which had till then enjoyed an enviable position in the market was suddenly faced with severe market erosion.

Jagdish Khattar, Managing Director, MUL, was a worried man. He was facing what was the biggest setback ever for the company. With most plans backfiring, Khattar seemed to be fighting a losing battle.

The Maruti-800 segment was facing demand erosion, Zen and its arch rival Santro were very close in terms of volumes, Esteem was losing ground, Baleno, Wagon-R and Alto were yet to prove themselves, while the Gypsy remained in its niche.

Despite the fact that MUL had the biggest range of products, the cheapest cars in the market, and a service network and cost structure better than anyone else, it had steadily lost its market share – from 82.62 per cent in 1998 to 52 per cent in 2000.

One of the biggest success sagas in Indian automobile history, the Maruti 800 started losing its sheen in the 1990s as newer players emerged in the market. The entry-level segment ceased to be the center of action as easy car finance availability and the lure of new cars made the Rs 3-lakh to Rs 4-lakh segment the most attractive one.

To tackle these problems, MUL adopted a two-pronged strategy. One, to introduce models; two, it decided to increase the number of variants rapidly, offering a new model with every increase of Rs 25000. As part of this, Baleno, Wagon-R and Alto were launched in quick succession.

MUL revamped its engines and took the 800 to semiurban and rural areas, to compensate for the declining urban sales. However, the engine revamp exercise for the 800 had pushed its price close to the base model of rival Daewoo's Matiz and MUL decided to play what it thought was its trump card price reduction.

MUL reduced the prices of Maruti 800 and Zen by about Rs 24,000 and Rs 51,000 respectively in December 1998. This resulted in a drop of Rs 3 billion in net profit for the year 1998-99. Khattar justified the price-cuts, saying that MUL wanted to make up for the increase in the 800's price due to higher sales tax figure for the period.

In early 2000, sales of the Maruti 800 stood at 5296 cars compared to the 11,000 plus cars it had been selling per month for the previous few years. MUL had no option but to again slash the prices of various models by Rs 25,000 to Rs 30,000 to bring back the sales to normal levels.

Towards the end of 2000, MUL again effected a price increase of between 0.3 to 2.5 per cent on its various models due to increase in the cost of production, raw material and other inputs. The company, however, decided to pass on only a part of the increase in cost to the customer.

All in all, with over 12 car manufacturers having a presence in the country in the late 1990s, with a total capacity of about 1,250,000 cars, MUL produced about 4,00,000 (33 per cent). Khattar perhaps rightly asked, "Tell me, if we have a market share of 50 per cent (plus) out of a capacity that is 33 per cent (of the industry), are we doing badly? Why don't you ask the others who together have a capacity of 8,00,000, but cannot match our sales?"

All said and done, MUL continued as the leader in early 2001. It still had early mover advantages. Khattar and MUL had survived.

> **The Learning**
>
> *Level-C:*
> - Re-assesses situations in light of changing priorities.
>
> *Level-B:*
> - Prepared to take calculated risks to achieve change.
>
> *Level-A:*
> - Takes a flexible approach, shifts focus as required.

Other themes covered: Business Focus, Planning and Organising.

3. K. M. Birla's Philosophy of Change

K. M. Birla who heads the Aditya Birla Group understands that due to technology, globalisation and opening of markets there is constant churn, competition and change. In such an environment, organisations have to radically transform themselves, not once or twice but continuously and many times over. At the broadest level, the topmost task is that of positioning an organisation along a permanent transformational track. He likes to quote Alvin Toffler who once wrote that, in the future people who wanted to stay ahead will have to learn, unlearn and relearn. It is often said that Birla's greatest strength is his understanding of people. Talking of the key challenges facing organisational leadership he once said, "People count. You can have the most forward-looking vision and strategy, but unless you have a passionate and committed team to execute it, you cannot translate your vision into reality". It is important to muster the emotional and intellectual equity of the people, and to gain their trust and commitment to the vision articulated by the organisation. Birla affirms that it is worthwhile to create intellectual ferment and constructive dissent so that people are not bound by the *status quo*, and mavericks are given space and free play. For him, the process of change is perhaps 90 per cent about leadership and only 10 per cent about managing.

Birla feels that in transformation, heterogeneity or diversity helps. A heterogeneous mix of people, though very difficult to lead, often helps in the process of change. As, he says, one needs bowlers, spinners and good wicket keepers just as much as the pinch hitters to become a winning team. "Altering the genetic coding, albeit carefully, can be a productive exercise" that can significantly improve the quality of constructive dissent and the quality of decision making, particularly in a period of rapid change. Bringing in people from outside cultures, people with different skill sets and a different vision, can be useful. The only thing to remember is that the diversity cannot compromise the need for the organisation to stay rooted to its core values.

Birla gives great importance to the ordinary worker who keeps the everyday operations moving. And they form the silent majority though not always visible. He believes that due focus on the top talent is necessary, but it is equally important to focus on that bulk of the organisation who make the day-to-day things happen. Their role in the process of change is critical. These people are involved in following the rules and they keep it moving ahead at a steady pace. An organisation cannot have everyone setting the rules. There is need for people who follow the rules, people who may not contribute in a significant way intellectually but who are happy to implement the rules diligently. Birla affirms, "Ignoring this segment of people in a process of change, I believe, can lead to organisational dehydration. For sustaining the transformation, you need to engage and recognise this quiet majority".

Globalisation puts a premium on how well an organisation can build a bridge between different cultures and geographies. People have to integrate with cultures that are foreign to it and practices that are new to them. Birla feels that efforts should go to create not an "Indian manager who works internationally" but a "global manager who happens to be Indian".

> **The Learning**
>
> *Level-C:*
> - Introduces new approaches and work methods for managing change.
>
> *Level-B:*
> - Prepared to take calculated risks to achieve change.
>
> *Level-A:*
> - Takes a flexible approach, shifts focus as required.

Other themes covered: Leadership, Planning and Organising.

Professional Improvement

2. Continuous Improvement/ Innovation

"This is our new one robot army! All our security worries will be over!"

Essentially continuous improvement is about involving the entire workforce in improving processes incrementally in a company. It is the process by which the radical innovations can be refined and improved. Along with the obvious performance benefits, continuous improvement has also proved to dramatically increase staff support for future radical change in companies. For continuous improvement, the high level strategic goals of a business must be linked with specific tasks and targets of the employees (this is often referred to as 'policy deployment'). Managements also need to develop skills to assess quickly which ideas will benefit the company and which will not.

With this competency:

One generates new ideas to improve existing approaches and create new opportunities; one is creative – thinks laterally and challenges assumptions; identifies learning from all experiences and applies it to new situations.

LEVELS OF PROFICIENCY
Proficiency Level C

"The boss feels we should know some sign language so we can communicate in the toughest situations!"

- Defines methods/procedures for capitalising on experience.
- Defines new standards for improving service or products.
- Uses innovation to improve efficiency and results.
- Explores new information channels for technology updating.
- Stimulates steady improvement in current processes.

> "Without change there is no innovation, creativity, or incentive for improvement. Those who initiate change will have a better opportunity to manage the change that is inevitable."
> – *William Pollard*

> "You have all the reason in the world to achieve your grandest dreams. Imagination plus innovation equals realisation."
> – *Denis Waitley*

> "If you're not failing every now and again, it's a sign you're not doing anything very innovative."
> – *Woody Allen*

Proficiency Level B

"Ha! I discern a certain pattern in these two images!"

- Identifies possibilities to do things differently.
- Creates opportunities to test new ideas.
- Thinks laterally and pragmatically.
- Challenges assumptions, questions existing processes.
- Shows creative vision.
- Combines different combinations to generate various options.
- Thinks outside the box.

"Innovation is the specific instrument of entrepreneurship – the act that endows resources with a new capacity to create wealth."
— *Peter F. Drucker*

"Innovation is not the product of logical thought, although the result is tied to logical structure."
— *Albert Einstein*

"Innovation is the whim of an elite before it becomes a need of the public."
— *Ludwig von Mises*

Proficiency Level A

"My third crash in a week? Just think officer, I am finally convinced now that I shouldn't drive!"

- Prepared to tackle unfamiliar areas.
- Prepared to handle tasks outside of own role.
- Builds on ideas of others.
- Gains positive learning from negative incidents.
- Designs, makes creative suggestions for new or improved processes.
- Identifies and follows up on opportunities.
- Takes an interest in activities outside direct responsibilities.
- Seeks to improve self, e.g., through further education.
- Adapts existing ideas to other circumstances.

> "It would be a terrific innovation if you could get your mind to stretch a little further than the next wisecrack."
>
> – *Katharine Hepburn*
>
> "Once again, this nation has said there are no dreams too large, no innovation unimaginable and no frontiers beyond our reach."
>
> – *John S. Herrington*

Case Studies

From the World of Business

1. Innovation at Wipro*

In July 2001, a technical team at Wipro Technologies (WT), the flagship company of Wipro, created workflow automation solutions for the publishing industry. This was a significant step as it resulted in a framework around which Wipro built a huge market for automation of business processes.

In November 2001, the workflow automation solutions were named Content Commerce. Initially, Wipro focused on the publishing industry but with the huge success of Content Commerce, the company decided to expand the solutions to other areas such as finance, insurance and manufacturing.

Wipro's management believed that innovation was essential to achieve growth and a competitive advantage. Innovation was one of the values in Wipro's vision statement. According to analysts, the deepset culture of innovation in Wipro gave it an edge over others in the knowledge-based industry.

The top management at Wipro believed that to achieve its goal of being among the top ten IT services companies in the world by 2005, it had to focus on offering innovative solutions to customers. The company always encouraged innovation in different parts of the organisation. After 2002 it became a corporation-wide initiative. Very soon Wipro was concentrating on innovative ideas in themes like Home Networking, Wireless Telecommunications and Workplace Collaboration.

Background

Wipro was established in 1945 under the name Western India Vegetable Products Limited in Maharashtra and commenced operations in 1946. In 1947, the company set up an oil mill and hydrogenated cooking medium plant at Amalner in Maharashtra for manufacturing vegetable ghee, edible oil and laundry soap.

---

* Adapted from ICMR cases/caselets; the original versions can be procured from ICMR/accessed on the ICMR website.

In 1966, Azim Hasham Premji became chairman of Wipro and charted an expansion plan for the company. This included diversification into manufacturing toiletries and baby care products. In 1975, the company diversified into hydraulic cylinders and fluid power components and its factory at Amalner was used for production of soaps, toiletries, and baby care products.

Wipro soon entered the lighting products market through Wipro Bulbs. In 1980, Wipro entered the IT industry with its subsidiary WT being established in Bangalore. In the 1980s, in the Indian Institute of Science (IISc) lab, the company's team developed India's first mini computer. It was the first Indian company to design and develop multi-processor systems in India, to design and manufacture mini computers and write a compiler. Subsequently, Wipro diversified into IT-related businesses such as IT peripherals.

By the mid 1990s, WT became the flagship company of the group. It was also one of the largest software exporters from India after Tata Consultancy Services and Infosys Technologies. Over the years, Wipro entered into various alliances with global IT majors. With increasing globalisation, Wipro started focusing more on the IT-related products and services.

Over the years, Wipro implemented various quality processes in its organisations to ensure high quality products and services. The company paid special attention to attaining high quality standards in WT and Wipro InfoTech so as to gain a global market share.

The Learning

Level-C:
- Defines new standards for improving service or products.

Level-B:
- Creates opportunities to test new ideas.

Other themes covered: Planning and Organizing, Business Focus.

2. Lessons from Nokia*

Nokia is the world's biggest mobile phone company and the reason can be attributed to its passion for betterment of its products, and strong desire to remain the world leader in the mobile-phone industry.

It is an industry that's all about innovation and Nokia has tackled the ultimate creative act. It has fostered a culture where innovation is built into the way the company operates.

The competition in this industry has been at full throttle for sometime. By the late nineties, it was clear that pushing the same old goods to the customers would not work. Handsets that are popular today will be out of fashion in the next six months or may be even before. Also, the number of customers were increasing at a brisk place and there were many more competitors in the race.

But Nokia stood up to the challenge. In 2001, Nokia launched 15 products. In 2002, it doubled that to 30 new products and launched even more products in the years that followed...

The life of its innovation goes on and on. The latest handsets from Nokia are equipped with features like a flashlight, rubberised case, thermometer, calorie counter, stopwatch, radio, etc.

But how does Nokia achieve all that? It believes that the raw material to successful innovation is talent. It's a result of the extraordinary intellectual and technical resources at Nokia's disposal. It's a combination of putting people in the right environment to generate ideas and giving them the power to make those ideas happen.

The R&D setup at Nokia was unique. While most large companies had centralised R&D facilities with tall hierarchical structures to facilitate strict control over processes and research, Nokia's R&D operations were scattered across the world in 69 sites and its 19,579 (as on December 2002) engineers, designers and sociologists were given complete freedom to operate and develop their own ideas, over and above their officially designated research projects. The

---

* Adapted from ICMR cases/caselets; the original versions can be procured from ICMR/accessed on the ICMR website.

structure was flat and most of the employees reported directly to the head of R&D. This was the creative pool of the company and the system worked wonders.

The Learning

Level-C:
- Uses innovation to improve efficiency and results.

Level-B:
- Identifies possibilities to do things differently.

Level-A:
- Prepared to tackle unfamiliar areas.

Other themes covered: Service Focus.

Recruitment – The CISCO Way*

In 1995, global networking major, Cisco, found that despite hiring an average of 1,000 people every three months during the year, the company still had hundreds of openings. The recruitment pressure further increased the following year.

When Cisco's sales soared to $ 6.4 billion in fiscal 1997 and profits to $ 1.4 billion, (a 53 per cent increase over the previous year), the company had to double its workforce and at the same time hire the best people.

The Cisco management needed to adopt innovative recruitment measures to get the best people and remain the leader in the internet era. Foremost among these was the first of its kind online recruitment called the 'Friends program'. Michael McNeal, Director, Corporate Employment said, "Friends is designed to put some grace into the hiring process." Cisco recruiters also began to target passive job seekers, who were content in their existing jobs.

Cisco maintained its lead in the global InfoTech industry, largely due to its streamlined and modernised recruitment policies. In 2001, the company recruited around 40-50 per

---

* Adapted from ICMR cases/caselets; the original versions can be procured from ICMR/accessed on the ICMR website.

cent of its employees through 'Make a friend@Cisco' online program and other such initiatives. It was the most innovative recruitment drive at the time and paid huge dividends.

Background

Cisco was founded in 1984 by a group of computer scientists at Stanford, who designed an operating software called IOS (Internet Operating System). This software could send streams of data from one computer to another, which was loaded into a box containing microprocessors specially designed for routing. This machine, called the router, made Cisco a hugely successful venture over the next two decades.

In 1985, the company started a customer support site from where customers could download software over FTP and also upgrade the downloaded software. It also provided technical support to its customers through emails.

Subsequently, Cisco installed a bug report database in its site. The database contained information about potential software problems to help customers and developers. It allowed customers to know whether a specific problem was unique and if not how other customers had solved it.

By 1991, Cisco's support centre was receiving over 3,000 calls a month which increased to 12,000 by 1992. To deal with the large volume of transactions, it built an online customer support system on its site. In 1993, Cisco installed an Internet-based system for large multinational corporate customers. The system allowed customers to post queries related to their problems. Cisco also installed a trigger function called the Bug Alert on its web site. The Bug Alert sent emails about software problems within 24 hours of their discovery.

Encouraged by the success of its customer support site in 1994, Cisco launched Cisco Information Online, a public website that offered not only company and product information but also technical and customer support to customers around the world.

The Learning

Level-C:
- Explores new information channels for technology updating.

Level-B:
- Identifies possibilities to do things differently.
- Creates opportunities to test new ideas.

Other themes covered: Business Focus, Planning and Organizing.

Professional Improvement

3. Personal Responsibility

*"How would I know its you sir, at this hour!
I was only doing my duty!"*

Personal responsibility is vital for any kind of success. It develops within a person when he exhibits enthusiasm, and energy to make things happen. He must have an element of zeal, an element of passion in himself, not only to complete the given tasks but also to accept new work. He should be willing to be the only champion for an idea. It is important that to complete his responsibilities, a person needs to be calm and composed under pressure. He should not rely too much on others and must have confidence in his abilities. He must abstain from delegating work that he can perform himself without any help.

With this competency:

An individual becomes fully responsible for the work assigned to him; he should realise that the onus lies on him to be accountable for the work, for his efforts and for ensuring that the outcomes are achieved.

LEVELS OF PROFICIENCY

Proficiency Level C

"Don't worry. I think we are effectively managing a high pressure situation!"

- Pursues the development of results, focusing on priorities and effectively managing pressure situations.
- Searches out alternative solutions in the face of problems and obstacles, maintaining self control and focus on objectives.
- Acts consistently with company values.
- Self-motivated.
- Rolls up sleeves and gets stuck in.
- Rises to challenges.
- Prepared to do routine tasks, and follows company procedures, when appropriate.

> "Stay committed to your decisions, but stay flexible in your approach."
> – *Tom Robbins*
>
> "It is easy to dodge our responsibilities, but we cannot dodge the consequences of dodging our responsibilities."
> – *Josiah Charles Stamp*
>
> "Nobody ever did, or ever will, escape the consequences of his choices."
> – *Alfred A. Montapert*

Personal Responsibility

Proficiency Level B

"I told the union it was good for all that I get to know things from the management perspective!"

- Desires to make things happen.
- Seizes opportunities and maintains a positive approach.
- Confidence in self, unafraid to speak up, even in face of conflict.
- Integrity, e.g., sticking to own values.

> "You are not only responsible for what you say, but also for what you do not say."
> – *Martin Luther*
>
> "Freedom is the will to be responsible to ourselves."
> – *Friedrich Nietzsche*
>
> "Responsibility is the price of greatness."
> – *Winston Churchill*

Proficiency Level A

"You two will be in charge here. I did not mean top management when I said you will be close to the 'source of all power'!"

- Recognises own limitations, knows when to hold back, utilising experience of others.
- Calm under pressure and emotionally controlled.
- Stands ground – shows tenacious approach.
- Persistent, even when people say no and remains optimistic.
- Bounces back from failure.
- Prepared to use own personal time to reach deadlines; balances own needs with needs of the company.

> "It is the responsibility of leadership to provide opportunity, and the responsibility of individuals to contribute."
> – *William Pollard*

> "I am free because I know that I alone am morally responsible for everything I do."
> – *Robert A. Heinlein*

Case Studies

From the World of Business

1. Responsibility to Shareholders – The Dhirubhai Way

This is the truly rags-to-riches story of a man who proved that entrepreneurs are born. This is the story of a man who rose from obscurity to create corporate history. Dhirajlal Hirachand Ambani (fondly called Dhirubhai) was born to Jamunaben and Hirachand Govardhandas Ambani, a lowly paid school teacher, in 1932, in Chorwad, a village in Saurashtra region of Gujarat. Dhirubhai Ambani was undoubtedly the greatest businessman ever produced by India in several respects. His achievements were not based on hard work done by his father and forefathers. He was a self-made man who had not attended even an ordinary college, but could teach a lesson or two in management to any professor at Harvard or Stanford. He was voted as the Indian Businessman of the Century by several surveys and polls.

Dhirubhai rose to dizzying heights from filling gas at a petrol pump to setting up the largest grassroot oil refinery in the world, from borrowing Rs 100 to buy clothes in order to go to Aden for a job to setting up the most modern textile mill in the country; and from being a member of a lower middle class Indian family to being a member of the *Forbes* list of the richest men in the world.

Dhirubhai always felt major responsibility towards the thousands of people who had invested in Reliance. After the banks turned him away for money, he had to look for support from the only other option – the public. Reliance came out with massive public issues which were real 'mega issues'. The pressure to do more, to succeed came from the support the public displayed time and again.

Dhirubhai took full responsibility for all his decisions. In return, he ensured that the price of Reliance shares kept appreciating, month after month, year after year. He knew as long as he kept moving, money would pour in. In order to better perform on his responsibilities, he introduced a concept that was alien to the Indian investors. He believed that most generous of dividends could not make a shareholder rich, but capital appreciation of his shares could. It took him almost half a decade to propagate this philosophy but once it took root, it changed the entire mindset of corporate India and its way of doing business.

An interesting example of Dhirubhai taking challenges head-on can be seen when the problem arose of posting innumerable share certificates, annual reports, and other correspondence to its family of investors. Not depending on India's weak postal department, Dhirubhai took the responsibility on his shoulders. Reliance decided to fly executives to smaller cities with mail as personal luggage which was then posted locally. Dhirubhai's most outstanding achievement was to introduce the equity cult to every small town in India. He is largely responsible for the reason that today in semiurban areas and small towns many people understand stocks and shares and read financial news.

Thus, Dhirubhai single-handedly energised the Indian capital market. Dhirubhai made Reliance India's most popular company. In 1977, Reliance had 58,000 investors. In 1988, when Reliance Petrochemicals went public, it attracted the world's second largest (after British Gas, which had 3.1 million shareholders) shareholder population of 1.6 million. By the end of 2002, before he died, Reliance had about 4 million shareholders.

The Learning

Level-C:
- Rises to challenges.

Level-B:
- Confidence in self, unafraid to speak up, even in face of conflict.

Level-A:
- Stands ground; tenacious approach.

Other themes covered: Business Focus, Leadership.

2. Aditya Vikram Birla: Investing in Quality

Aditya Vikram Birla was a visionary who left an indelible imprint on the nation and on corporate leadership. He made an enormous direct contribution to business, the economy and the community, and this was recognised in his lifetime.

As 'Profit' was the cornerstone of the Company's management philosophy and in a seller's market, consumers had no choice but to tolerate the shoddiness of Birla products. Ghanshyam Das (GD) Birla was a shrewd businessman, who had grown up in an era of shortages and didn't believe in quality. Aditya realised it was high time that he changed this tradition. He could foresee the changes emerging in the market. Aditya took the onus on his shoulders and soon placed great importance on the issue of quality.

In the bazaar, a cliché had been born: Birlas look after shareholders; the Tatas, consumers. Aditya took a longer view on quality than GD and tried to turn the cliché on its head. But it was not an easy road to take. The company did not have a culture to invest for distant returns.

Aditya was to say later, "Earlier we used to compromise on quality machinery. I recognised that it is better to spend a little extra for better machinery because it pays in the longer run. If the machinery is good, the product is good, sales are good and profitability is good... Now we produce the best aluminium and the best insulators. In our category of suiting we are the best. In carbon black we are the best both in India and abroad and you can check this with our competitors in Indonesia. In acrylic fibre and in Sodium phosphate we are the best. In filament yarn, we are not the best but one of the best."

The efforts of Aditya did pay off and his factories began picking up awards and getting more recognition. In 1974, for example, Grasim's, Harihar Rayon grade pulp plant received the Sir P.C. Roy award for the development of indigenous technology. Some years later, Grasim built a $7 million viscose staple fibre plant in Korea, whose production the Japanese Synthetic Textile Inspection Institution declared was "equal to Japanese export products". In 1979, a team of World Bank experts highlighted the efficiency of Indo-phil

Textile Mills' textile machinery. Subsequently, in October 1994, Indo-Gulf became the first Indian Fertilizer manufacturer to receive ISO 9002 certification. Such recognition meant a lot to Aditya.

The Learning

Level-C:
- Rises to challenges.
- Self-motivated.

Level-B:
- Desires to make things happen.

Level-A:
- Recognises own limitations and knows when to hold back, utilising experience of others.

Other themes covered: Business Focus, Leadership

Professional Improvement

4. Technical Skills

"This is no ordinary remote. It can shut down all the machines in the neighbourhood!"

Technical skills refer to the ability of a person to effectively apply the knowledge, gathered over the years, within a particular area of expertise. Having sound knowledge is not enough – only protected usable knowledge can create wealth. Leaders have to maintain a high level of awareness and expertise in their own subject area. Technological literacy is not the same as technical competency. Technically trained people have a high level of knowledge and skill related to one or more specific technologies or technical areas.

With this competency:

One maintains a high level of knowledge and expertise in own subject area and applies this to new situations; understands technical aspects of related areas; and develops both breadth and depth of technical knowledge.

LEVELS OF PROFICIENCY
Proficiency Level C

"Imagine, in the whole organisation we will be the only ones with this special skill!"

- Demonstrates authoritative sources of specific know-how in own area.
- Provides strategic direction in own area of expertise; looks for new information on best practices and possible developments in own field of expertise.
- Develops new skills in new functions/areas.
- Has a depth and breadth of understanding in more than one specialty area.

> "All of the top achievers I know are life-long learners... Looking for new skills, insights, and ideas. If they're not learning, they're not growing... not moving toward excellence."
> – *Denis Waitley*

Technical Skills

Proficiency Level B

"You call that a technical solution to an alarming problem??"

- Understands technical and/or marketing aspects of related areas.
- Able to identify appropriate technical solutions.
- Maintains and regularly updates knowledge of processes, products and principles in own area.
- Shows broad understanding of own area of expertise, acts as a key source of expertise in this field.

> "The five steps in teaching an employee new skills are preparation, explanation, showing, observation and supervision."
> – *Bruce Barton*
>
> "Education is not the piling on of learning, information, data, facts, skills, or abilities – that's training or instruction – but is rather making visible what is hidden as a seed."
> – *Thomas More*

Proficiency Level A

"We are settling our debate of specialist vs. generalist, once and for all!!"

- Makes the effort to learn and read/learn about new approaches.
- Applies technical knowledge to new situations.
- Answers technical queries accurately.
- Understands the basic theories, practices and procedures in own area.
- Has the knowledge and/or practical skills to work on a range of activities.
- Demonstrates specialist knowledge & skills.
- SAP/PC knowledge, skills.
- Specialist focus, e.g., health and safety, wears safety equipment, vigilant in security issues.
- Takes a generalist vs. specialist approach where appropriate.

"Some people give time, some money, some their skills and connections, some literally give their life's blood. But everyone has something to give."
– *Barbara Bush*

"A winner is someone who recognises his God-given talents, works his tail off to develop them into skills, and uses these skills to accomplish his goals."
– *Larry Bird*

"It is one of the chief skills of the philosopher not to occupy himself with questions which do not concern him."
– *Ludwig Wittgenstein*

Case Studies

1. Sony Corporation – Managing a Global Corporation*

Sony's ability to innovate and become a household brand globally has been remarkable. Founder Masaru Ibuka once remarked, "We shall welcome technical difficulties and focus on highly sophisticated technical products that have great usefulness for society, regardless of the quantity involved; we shall place our main emphasis on ability, performance, and personal character so that each individual can show the best in ability and skill."

Sony also had a special place among Japanese companies due to the relatively outgoing nature, flamboyant leadership, and global mindset of its top executives.

Morita, a co-founder of the company who died in October 1999, was not only one of the best known business personalities in the world, but also an international ambassador for the Japanese business community. The next Chairman, Nobuyuki Idei (Idei), was also a firm believer in globalisation. In April 2003, Idei stunned investors by announcing that the consumer-electronics giant had suffered a quarterly loss of about $1 billion. Sony's share price plunged nearly 25 per cent in two days.

Profit margins on electronics products had plunged to around 1 per cent, down from 10 per cent a decade ago. With easily available components, other players were also offering CD players, digital cameras, and other gadgets which became commodities almost as soon as they hit the market.

In April 2003, Idei announced he would cut 20,000 jobs, close down plants, and overhaul the ailing electronics division. But he also gave the approval to invest $4.5 billion in the development of new chips, including a super high-powered microprocessor for Sony's next generation PlayStation game console. Sony was not giving up its innovative ways. And thus came a year later.

---

* Adapted from ICMR cases/caselets; the original versions can be procured from ICMR/accessed on the ICMR website.

In 2004, Sony, the world's number one consumer electronics firm, recorded a revenue of $72 billion and a net profit of $851 million. The company made a host of other products, including PCs, digital cameras, Walkman stereos, semiconductors, TVs, stereos, and other consumer electronics products. Sony's entertainment businesses included recorded music and videos (Epic and Columbia), motion pictures, DVDs, and TV programming (Columbia TriStar). Sony's PlayStation 2 dominated the game console market with about 70 per cent of global sales (Nintendo's GameCube and Microsoft's Xbox controlled about 15 per cent each).

Background

Morita, who had been expected to join his family's *sake*-brewing business, had different ideas. He teamed up with Masaru Ibuka and Tamon Maeda to set up Tokyo Tsushin Kogyo Kabushiki Kaisha (Tokyo Telecommunications Engg. Co.) in 1946. The high ideals of the founders were documented in the founding prospectus:

"The establishment of an ideal factory – free, dynamic and pleasant, where technical personnel of sincere motivation can exercise their technological skills to the highest level."

The company began by manufacturing telecommunication and measuring equipment. Later, it moved into tape recorders and then transistor radios.

When Tokyo Tsushin Kogyo proposed a change in name to Sony, the company's bank objected. There was logic in its objection. The company's name had made a mark after ten years and a change could upset everything, particularly the goodwill created.

Morita argued that for global expansion, it was necessary to have a name, which could be pronounced easily in foreign lands. The company was renamed Sony in 1958.

Sony set up a sales subsidiary in the U.S. in 1960. The company's shares were listed on the New York Stock Exchange in 1970. In 1972, Sony became the first Japanese company to set up manufacturing facilities in the U.S.

Sony rapidly established its reputation as a highly innovative company, quite unlike many of its Japanese counterparts. The founders demonstrated their commitment to innovation by attaching less importance to market research than other companies. Many of Sony's products when launched, did not have any proven demand and were more like maverick ideas given shape.

Sony suffered a setback in 1975, when its Betamax Video Cassette Recorder failed. But the turning point came in 1979, when Sony launched the Walkman, which became a huge success. Sony continued its innovation spree, developing the compact disc player, camcorder, home movie electronic equipment, and the 3.5-inch floppy disk in the early 1980s.

In response to adverse currency rates and competition worldwide, Sony began to diversify beyond consumer electronics and decided to move production to other countries. By the mid 1980s, Sony had set up subsidiaries in the UK, Germany, and France. Sony also subsequently entered Australia, Hong Kong, and Panama. Besides, it appointed distributors and wholesalers in other parts of the world. Sony made two important acquisitions in the U.S. in the late 1980s – CBS Records (1988) and Columbia Pictures (1989) spending over $7 billion.

The Learning

Level-C:
- Develops new products and skills in new areas and functions.

Level-B:
- Maintains and regularly updates knowledge of processes, products, and principles in own area.

Level-A:
- Interested and committed to expanding depth and breadth of technical knowledge.

Other themes covered: Business Focus, Service Focus.

2. Bill Gates: His Technical Leadership*

In 2004, Microsoft – world's largest computer software company was at the crossroads. Growth had slowed down, while the competitive environment was changing. Longhorn, Microsoft's new operating system had been delayed. The Linux threat was intensifying. A new Microsoft seemed to be evolving under the joint leadership of Bill Gates (Gates) and Steve Ballmer (Ballmer). Could Microsoft maintain its awesome competitive position in the global software industry? That was the issue which analysts debated as 2004 drew to a close.

In the early 1970s, the computer industry focused on hardware. Software was considered less important. However, Gates and Paul Allen had their own vision of what software could become. They wanted to develop software that would make personal computers (PCs) an all-purpose machine. This was an ambitious goal because PC software did not exist at the time. Indeed, there were no PCs. Effectively, two young men were trying to build a software business when the software industry itself did not exist. But the bet paid off. By 1990, Microsoft had become the undisputed leader of the software revolution. Software dictated the pace of innovation in the industry. Software was also hugely profitable unlike hardware, where most manufacturers struggled to earn thin margins in the face of intense competition.

Microsoft was valued at over $7 billion, grossing over $1 billion a year by 1990, with almost half a billion dollars in cash and no debt. With a 36 per cent ownership of the company, Gates was personally worth more than $2 billion.

A major turning point came when Microsoft unleashed a new operating system – Windows 3.0 of which most analysts had predicted an early demise, especially when IBM refused to adopt it. But by May 1991, a year after it was introduced, Windows 3.0 had sold a million units, more than the entire Apple Macintosh sales since its inception in January 1984.

---

* Adapted from ICMR cases/caselets; the original versions can be procured from ICMR/accessed on the ICMR website.

By the start of 1992, Microsoft was valued at more than $22 billion, making Gates, with more than $7 billion worth of stock, the richest person in America.

The rest of the 1990s were glorious years for Microsoft, financially. By 1999, it was generating revenues of $19.75 billion and profits of $7.79 billion. Its workforce had grown by the end of the 1990s to 31,575.

By early 2001, growth slowed down for Microsoft. The company found it difficult to come up with radically new products despite investing heavily on R&D. The anti-trust proceedings occupied much of the attention of Microsoft during the period 1998-2002. Sensing the need to present a new image to the general public and to concentrate on technology issues, Gates made Ballmer (his old friend and long time colleague) the CEO in 2000. Gates, however, continued to play a significant role. By 2004, Gates seemed to be enjoying himself, dividing his time over Microsoft and philanthropic activities. By all accounts, Gates was a more mellowed person.

Gates' Management Style

Gates had traditionally managed Microsoft with a few key business principles in mind. He believed in keeping head count low, minimising costs, and centralising as much of the operation as possible. Gates wanted everyone to surpass their potential. These became the defining features of Microsoft's start-up culture. A firm believer in 'stretch', he had attempted to keep the organisation small and unbureaucratic.

Gates was greatly concerned that Microsoft might one day resemble an unwieldy conglomerate more than a start-up. He was firmly opposed to many practices common in large companies. Among the barred practices were, new levels of management, job titles, and long vacations.

Introducing such initiatives, Gates believed, would only encourage employees to become complacent and laid back. Even into the early 1990s, Microsoft's operations were not too complicated to manage. The company was essentially a two-product company: operating systems and software applications for personal computers. Microsoft continued to avoid bureaucracy. Most decisions were made by Gates and Ballmer. If people connected with them on e-mail, they typically got a response the same day.

Gates had shaped a highly competitive environment inside the company. His temper was legendary.

The praise he sometimes offered was usually brief and unemotional. Time was too precious he felt, to waste on laudatory speeches. If Microsoft was going to change the world, his employees had to work hard and excel. Only in a confrontational environment would that happen. For Gates, confrontation was something positive and desirable.

Right from Microsoft's startup days, Gates had been very much a hands-on manager, prepared to get involved in various aspects of the company. Despite the powers he enjoyed, Gates had shown a tremendous ability to remain flexible and learn from his mistakes. Indeed, one of Gates' strength has been his willingness to re-invent the company over and over again. Gates shifted product strategies, sometimes overnight. The most famous example was his decision in the mid 1990s to make sure that all Microsoft products were web enabled. Microsoft's executives recalled the Windows 95 launch and how a month later, the focus shifted to how Microsoft had to re-invent itself to become webcentric. By successfully integrating Microsoft's products and making them more user-friendly, Gates realised the potential to generate a sustainable competitive advantage. No other company could offer such a wide array of software products. Gates believed that the more Microsoft's products interacted with one another, the more valuable would be the company's total offering. Despite the anti-trust proceedings and complaints from other firms about anti-competitive practices, Gates persisted with this vision.

The Learning

Level-C:
- Takes risk-mitigation measures and encourages others to take risks in a controlled manner.

Level-B:
- Uses all formal and informal channels to get the required information.

Level-A:
- Understands the need to make timely decisions.

Other themes covered: Business Focus, Leadership, Service Focus.

Professional Improvement

5. Initiative and Proactivity

"I am taking this Restricted Area Notice off as it will attract more attention to our kitchen than we want!"

Proactivity is one of the most popular management buzzwords to come from the 1990s. Yet there are a number of definitions of what it means to be proactive. Many would argue that being proactive means to take action on an issue before being asked. Stephen Covey, who has "be proactive" as the first of his famous "7 Habits of Highly Effective People", defines proactivity as more than merely taking the initiative but focuses on "response-ability" – the ability and freedom to choose our response to a stimulus.

With this competency:

One captures opportunities and takes the initiative; anticipates situations rather than awaiting their evolution, taking action promptly to resolve a situation, including actions and outcomes.

Initiative and Proactivity

LEVELS OF PROFICIENCY
Proficiency Level C

"What do you mean you did not hire any staff because HR was not listed on the business start-up plan?"

- Researches and mobilises the necessary resources to reach new objectives.
- Assumes necessary risks to improve results.
- Proposes new development opportunities for the organisation.

> 'The people who get on in this world are the people who get up and look for the circumstances they want and if they can't find them, make them."
> – *George Bernard Shaw*

Proficiency Level B

"It does not matter if we are not ready. I put this up now to preempt our rivals!"

- Identifies and acts on opportunities.
- Takes ownership for whole situation including actions and the outcome.
- Commits to taking a definite set of actions.

> "The future belongs to those who see possibilities before they become obvious."
> *– John Scully*
>
> "The pessimist sees difficulty in every opportunity. The optimist sees the opportunity in every difficulty."
> *– Sir Winston Churchill*

Proficiency Level A

"I am ready with emergency escape plan from this high rise building!"

- Is proactive – anticipates what is required and does it.
- Uses initiative to anticipate and resolve situations.
- Recognises urgent situations and takes action promptly.

"The man who can drive himself further once the effort gets painful is the man who will win."
– ***Roger Bannister***

"To him who is determined it remains only an act."
– ***Italian Proverb***

Case Studies

From the World of Business

1. Environmental Hero – Tulsi Kanti

For those working in sustainable development the name Suzlon is familiar. But not many know the story of its founder Tulsi Kanti who was honoured as 'Hero for the Environment' by *Time Magazine* in October 2007. Tulsi Kanti is an entrepreneur who is also responsible to society and the natural environment. He wants to pay back his debts to nature. Two incidents changed his life and gave him a clear vision of his destiny.

The first came with his electricity bills, back in 1994-95. The young engineer's fledgling textile company, Suzlon was just taking off as planned. His new line of polyester yarns was doing well, but India's shaky power grid and the rising cost of electricity offset any profits. Though constantly innovating, the unpredictability of power was a constant worry. Disgusted with the situation, Tulsi Kanti decided to generate his own power. After a few years of research, he settled on wind power, buying two turbines to provide his energy needs. The initial cost was steep, but the company headquartered in the western Indian city of Pune, was no longer buffeted by the spiralling cost of fossil fuels. Kanti soon turned advocate for renewable energy solutions and advised industrialist friends to seriously consider such renewable energy as an option.

The second turning point came in early 2000. While traveling he read a report on global warming predicting that without a radical decrease in the world's carbon emissions, several attractive destinations like the Maldives would be under water by 2050. It was then that Kanti realised his destiny lay far beyond the latest advances in synthetic fibers. He could easily foresee that a large developing country could not go forward on limited fossil fuels in the model of the developed industrialised world.

If wind was the answer to Suzlon's energy needs, asked Kanti, then why couldn't it fuel the growth of other industries? By 2001 Suzlon had sold off its textile manufacturing and plunged into the relatively new field of wind-turbine generators. Today, with factories on four continents and wind farms across Asia, Suzlon is the fourth largest wind-turbine maker in the world, with annual revenues of $850 million. With the price of oil hovering around $80-90 a barrel, Kanti ably supported by his brothers, is all the more convinced that wind is the energy of the future and that Suzlon will help launch the industry into the mainstream. "Yes, green business is good business," says Kanti. "But it's not just about making money. It's about being responsible." Suzlon's main factory, in the southeastern city of Pondicherry, runs exclusively on wind power. Rainwater is collected to tend the lush grounds, and the factory was constructed keeping local environment and ecological considerations in view.

The decision to shift to a new sector like wind energy was thus a very brave one. The industry was in the dumps as it had been given a bad name by unscrupulous companies that lured customers with the bait of tax breaks. Many projects were ill conceived, often left incomplete with no maintenance or service support to speak of. Banks became wary of such proposals and stopped lending for wind power projects.

The brothers saw the opportunity for a producer not only to build the wind turbine but to provide maintenance and service support and even operation. Selling some family property, the Kantis put together $600,000 as seed capital to start Suzlon. They shopped around for technology in Europe but no one was willing to give it without having an equity stake in the venture. Finally they found a German company that agreed to go with them. And that was the beginning...

BTM Consult ApS, a renewable energy consultancy in Denmark, predicts that the global installed capacity for wind power will go up to 124,000 megawatts by 2009. Kanti is positioning Suzlon to get a fair chunk of that growth by being a low-cost producer and is collecting engineering talent so Suzlon can continually improve technology.

> **The Learning**
>
> ***Level-C:***
> - Assumes necessary risks to improve results.
>
> ***Level-B:***
> - Takes ownership for whole situation including actions and the outcome.
>
> ***Level-A:***
> - Proactive; anticipates what is required and does it.

Other themes covered: Business Focus.

2. Deepak Puri: The Moser Baer Story

Deepak Puri, chairman and managing director of Moser Baer, is an example of perseverance and vision in the modern business world. He faced a series of setbacks in the 40 years of his business life but he never quit.

He never complained or looked for excuses; he tried to find solutions. If he had problems at the Indian ports, he set up his own supply chain. He tried to sort out his own power shortage problems.

With a masters in mechanical engineering from the Imperial College of Science and Technology, London, UK, Deepak started his business career from Kolkata. His first factory – Metal Industries Pvt. Ltd., – manufactured aluminum wires and pipes and AC conductors. But labour militancy forced him to shut down his factory.

This did not deter him. He started a second business – this one was about manufacturing time recording devices for the banking industry. But, before Deepak could even settle down, the militant labour union members stormed into his unit and damaged his machines. His two major attempts to do business did not result in success.

He faced protests at his plant but that did not bother him. Only when they actually *gheraoed* his home, he decided to move out.

Deepak was down but not out and he was ready for the third attempt. It was pure chance. He knew nothing about floppies in those days. He had gone to Mumbai to a friend's office. Those were the days of power shortage in Mumbai and people used to practice self-regulated power shedding. They switched off their electrical power voluntarily in their offices and houses.

When he entered his friend's office, he was fanning himself with a newspaper. "So, I picked up the first object I came across to fan myself with – an 8-inch square black object. But before I could begin fanning myself with it, my friend grabbed it back! It was a floppy disk. Believe me, I knew nothing about it or its data storage capacity." Deepak fired a hundred questions. He had just spotted a business opportunity.

Wasting no time, he flew to California to talk to Xidex, then the largest manufacturer of data storage media in the world. India was not a known country, at least on the technology front in those days. But the enthusiasm and conviction that Deepak brought to the table, impressed Xidex to partner with him. Thus, Moser Baer came into being in 1983.

The company, which started with 8-inch and 5.5-inch disks, today ranks among the top three optical and magnetic storage devices (CDs, DVDs, CD-Rs, CD-RWs and Lightscribe CD-Rs) in the world. Moser Baer stands for technology that matches the best in the world.

In R&D, it has set many industry benchmarks. It is the lowest cost optical media manufacturer in the world and has a human resource pool that is proud of every disk that leaves its facilities, with the 'Made in India' stamp, flashing on it.

So, what keeps them at the head of the line and prevents them from stagnating? Rao, an analyst from Frost & Sullivan, a leading business consulting firm that offers market research and analysis, says: "They keep on attempting to improve themselves. When their products start maturing or declining, they are ready with the next one." When the floppies went out, they moved on to CDs and when CDs were stagnating, they moved on to DVDs, which are now in the growth phase. It is obvious that when the DVDs go into the next phase of maturity, they will be ready with the next product. To this day, Deepak keeps on thinking ahead – this time to make Moser Baer an all-encompassing technology company, which will last a 100 years!

The Learning

Level-C:
- Proposes new development opportunities for the organisation.

Level-B:
- Takes ownership for whole situation including actions and the outcome.

Level-A:
- Proactive; anticipates what is required and does it.

Other themes covered: Business Focus.

3. Azim Hasham Premji: Wipro's Visionary Leader

This case discusses the overall quality initiatives taken by Wipro under Azim Hasham Premji. Wipro had always paid attention to the quality of its products and services. In 2001, the company successfully acquired the Six Sigma certification and also became the first company to be affirmed for the SEI-CMM (Capability Maturity Model) level 5 in the world. The same year, Wipro received the TL 9000 certification for the implementation of telecom products and the Bluetooth qualification from the Bluetooth Qualification Body (BQB).

These certifications helped the company products become defect free and it also resulted in enhanced customer satisfaction. But Premji was always worried about the high attrition rate that had plagued the software industry. Apprehensive that his talented technical personnel would leave the organisation, he decided to integrate business development with people development.

Premji decided to get Wipro a PCMM (People Capability Maturity Model) certification. PCMM implementation helped the software company to attract, develop, motivate, organise, and retain talented people for improving the software development capability of the organisation. The PCMM model contains a set of inter-related practices which at each maturity level transforms the capability of the organisation in managing the workforce.

This step enabled Wipro to provide its employees with better training and hands-on experiences. Premji felt that the certification would go a long way in helping Wipro integrate its human resources with its strategic objectives and organisational goals. He knew that the employees would feel more involved in the processes of the company and become more committed towards the company. This turned out to be a vital strategic decision, as the company rose quickly to become a big player in IT.

The measures also made the company, with Premji's foresight become better equipped to withstand the global slowdown in the early 21st century. He took Wipro to a position where it could adapt better to the rapid changes in the Indian information technology industry.

The Learning

Level-C:
- Researches and mobilises the necessary resources to reach new objectives.

Level-B:
- Commits to taking a definite set of actions.

Level-A:
- Proactive; anticipates what is required and does it.

Other themes covered: Business Focus, Service Focus, Leadership.

Competencies for CEOs

Some Exclusive Competencies for CEOs

INTELLECTUAL QUALITIES

1. Conceptual Understanding & Integration

Definition:
Connects with Board directors and translates their ideas into workable plans at company level.

Competency Behaviours:
- Sees the broader picture of organisational plans through understanding the directions and expectations of top management.
- Knows the intent and agenda of top management and translates their ideas into comprehensive and implementable plans at company level.
- Represents top management effectively by communicating their messages and taking into account the context, priorities, and local culture.
- Explains high-level directions/concepts and aligns company goals with them.
- Proactively responds to Board with sensible plans under uncertain work conditions, despite incomplete information.

Related Competencies
- Business knowledge
- Industry understanding
- Organisation understanding
- Information-search skills

Negative Competency Behaviours
- Takes things literally.
- Cascades ideas in a dogmatic way.
- Changes direction to accommodate own agenda.
- Waits for orders and instructions.

2. Strategic Planning & Organising

Definition:
Analyses business demands, formulates strategies, and communicates for commitment and actions.

Competency Behaviours:
- Visualises strategies as images, that show milestones for a 1- to 3-year (or more) performance period.
- Creates road maps and real work for others to perform.
- Identifies trends and upcoming demands, and communicates to generate work goals and plans for business growth.
- Makes meaning out of ambiguous and changing situations.
- Sets targets and makes amendments to stay in tune or ahead of external market changes.

Related Competencies
- Intellectual versatility
- Research
- Model-building skills

Negative Competency Behaviours
- Looks at short-term plans.
- Focuses on immediate problems.
- Visions in one-track manner.
- Sets only yearly or short-term goals.
- Not interested in external market conditions.
- Waits for orders and instructions.

ADAPTABLE QUALITIES

3. Versatile Leadership

Definition:
Manages diversity and change, creates climate for continuous improvement, and demonstrates high moral standards and integrity in all matters.

Competency Behaviours:
- Adjusts well to first-time experience situations and acts in effective ways for positive impact, without damaging organisational brand image.
- Encourages staff to voice out and accept diverse views and opinions.
- Adapts quickly to different cultures and etiquettes while upholding moral standards and integrity.
- Is versatile in learning and performing in new fields beyond own areas of responsibility.
- Manages relationships with tact and sensitivity to different people needs and preferences.

Related Competencies
- Self-knowledge
- Relationship-building skills
- Feedback skills
- Presentation skills

Negative Competency Behaviours
- Promises without consulting others.
- Insensitive to other's feelings.
- Refuses to understand and adapt.
- Protects status quo and unwilling to move from comfort zone.
- Shuts people off.

Pragmatic Qualities

4. Creative Implementation

Definition:
Engages fresh and different approaches to generate ideas and solutions, anticipates obstacles and responds forthrightly, and takes risks and evaluates results for mid- to long-term profits/benefits.

Competency Behaviours:
- Shows a good balance of broad breadth and in-depth technical and marketing knowledge.
- Thinks matters and decisions through thoroughly and checks own assumptions and logic.
- Formulates various business scenarios that accommodate different dynamic human factors.
- Understands the rationale of rules and policy and makes effort to change them when necessary.
- Manages conflicting goals (e.g., expand new businesses but reduce costs of SGA) for long-term benefits.
- Shows basic knowledge in legal, public relations, and finance.

"What the boss means is that within five years all major functions will be outsourced and there will be only five of us left in the corporate office!"

Related Competencies
- Project management skills
- Subject matter knowledge
- Goal-setting abilities
- Cost-benefit analysis skills
- Writing skills

Negative Competency Behaviours
- Plans ahead with one-sided view.
- Whimsical in judgment and a poor listener.
- Takes rules and policies as permanent and unchangeable.
- Sees conflicting goals as not manageable.

ACHIEVEMENT-ORIENTED QUALITIES

5. Building High-Impact Teams

Definition:
Involves diverse workgroups to align to overall goals, identifies strengths and weaknesses of staff, and works with them on their performance growth.

Competency Behaviours:
- Shows initiative to lead and guide members in both normal and difficult times.
- Understands details and knows what all members should do to attain results.
- Motivates people through clear targets and directions.
- Is keen to learn from experts and professionals and draw from their ideas and contributions.

Related Competencies
- Career development understanding
- Coaching/mentoring skills
- Counseling skills
- Consulting skills

Negative Competency Behaviours
- Micro-manages all matters.
- Does not delegate.
- Instructs more often than necessary.
- Does not see benefit of professional training & development for staff.

6. Performance Management

Definition:
Focuses on goals, mobilises necessary resources to achieve results, and takes ownership for whole situation including actions, outcomes, and consequences.

Competency Behaviours:
- Takes concrete actions to achieve agreed results.
- Takes personal responsibility for results and consequences.
- Manages critical incidents and is not bogged down by the day-to-day operational demands.
- Recognises mistakes, learns from them, and does not repeat them as far as possible.

"No I did not forget his ears! You told me that the outgoing chairman was a poor listener!"

Related Competencies
- Project management skills
- Subject matter understanding
- Goal-setting skills
- Cost-benefit analysis skills
- Writing skills

Negative Competency Behaviours
- Judges and refuses to listen.
- Does not learn from experts.
- Plans ahead with one-sided view.
- Takes rules and policies as permanent and unchangeable.
- Sees conflicting goals and pressures as not manageable.

References

Books & periodicals:

American Compensation Association (1996). *Raising the Bar: Using Competencies to Enhance Employee Performance.* Scottsdale, AZ: ACA.

Antonacopoulou, Elena & Fitzgerald, Louise (1996). Reframing competency in management development. *Human Resource Management Journal,* 6(1), 27-48.

Aurther Anderson, *Best Practices,* Simon & Schuster, London, 1998.

Austin, James, & Villanova, Peter (1992). The criterion problem. *Journal of Applied Psychology,* 77 (6), 836-874.

Austin, James, Klimoski, Richard, & Hunt, Steven (1996). Dilemmatics in public sector assessment: A framework for developing and evaluating selection systems. *Human Performance,* 9 (3), 177-198.

Barrett, G.V. (1994, January). Empirical data say it all. *American Psychologist,* 69-71.

Boyatzis, R. E. (1982). *The Competent Manager: A Model for Effective Performance.* New York: John Wiley and Sons.

Boyatzis, R. E. (1994, January). Rendering unto competence the things that are competent. *American Psychologist,* 64-66.

Braithewaite, Valerie (1994). Beyond Rokeach's equality-freedom model: Two dimensional values in a one-dimensional world. *Journal of Social Issues,* 50 (4), 67-94.

Bryson, John M. (1995). *Strategic Planning for Public and Nonprofit Organizations: A Guide to Strengthening and Maintaining Organizational Achievement.* San Francisco: Jossey-Bass.

Carroll, J. D. (1997). The warfare on and over American government in Waldonian perspective. *Public Administration Review,* 57(3), 200-210.

Chakraborty, S.K., *Managerial Transformation by Value*, Sage Publications, 1993.

Cowan, J.J. (1994, January). Barrett and Depinet versus McClelland. *American Psychologist*, p. 64.

Czarnecki, A. (1995, February 27). Some HRIS will link competencies with compensation and performance; no matter how you do it, it's still a lot of work. *Canadian HR Reporter*, 13-15.

Denhardt, Robert B. (1993). *The Pursuit of Significance: Strategies for Success in Public Organizations*. Belmont, CA: Wadsworth Publishing.

Donnellon, Anne & Kolb, Deborah (1994). Constructive for whom? The fate of diversity disputes in organizations. *Journal of Social Issues*, 50(1), 139-155.

Dror, Yehezkel (1997). Delta-type senior civil service for the 21st century. *International Review of Administrative Sciences* 63 (1) 7-23.

Drucker, Peter F, *Management Challenges for the 21st Century*, Butterworth-Heineman, Oxford, U.K., 2000.

Drucker, Peter F, *The Practice of Management*, Mercury Books, 1962.

Dubois, D. D. (1993). *Competency-based performance improvement: A strategy for organizational change*. Amherst: HRD Press Inc.

Dubois, David D. (1996). *The Executive's Guide to Competency-Based Performance Improvement*. Amherst MA: HRD Press Inc.

Flanagan, John, *Psychological Review*, Vol. 51, No. 4, 1954.

Fogg, C. D. (1994). *Team-Based Strategic Planning*. New York: Amacom.

Forcese, Dennis, P., and Richer, Stephen (1973). *Social Research Methods*, p. 38.

Furnham, A. (1990, June). A question of competency. *Personnel Management*, p. 37.

Ghosal, Sumantra and Bartlett, Christopher A, *The Individualized Corporation*, A. Harper Business Book, 1997.

Hendry I., and Maggio E. (1996, May). Tracking success: is competency-based human resources management an effective strategy or simply flavour of the month? *Benefits Canada*, N. 71.

Jacobs, R. (1989). Getting the measure of management competence. *Personnel Management*, June, 32-37.

Johns, Gary (1993). Constraints on the adoption of psychology-based personnel practices: Lessons from organizational innovation. *Personnel Psychology*, 46. 569-592.

Kalam, A.P.J. Abdul with Pillai, Sivathanu A., *Envisioning an Empowered Nation*, Tata McGraw-Hill Publishing Co. Ltd., New Delhi, 2004.

Kerr, Marjory R. (1995). Tacit knowledge as a predictor of managerial success: A field study. *Canadian Journal of Behavioural Science* 27 (1), 36-51.

Kotter, John P., *Making Change Happen, Leader to Leader*, The Drucker Foundation, New York, U.S.A., 1999.

Lado, A. and Wilson, M. (1994, Vol 19, No. 4). Human resource systems and sustained competitive advantage: a competency-based perspective. *Academy of Management Review*, 699-727.

Lewis, J. (1996, February 26). "What makes competency-based programs succeed? *Canadian HR Reporter*, p. 2.

Lowe, Rosemary (1993). Master's programs in industrial-organizational psychology: Current status and a call for action. *Professional Psychology: Research and Practice*, 24(1), 27-34.

Maor, Moshe & Stevens, Handley (1997). Measuring the impact of New Public Management and European Union on recruitment and training in the UK civil service. *Public Administration*, 75, 531-551.

Margerison and McCann, 1985 – *How to Lead a Winning Team*, MCB University Press, Bradford; 1989 – *How to Improve Team Management*, MCB.

McClelland D.C. (1994, January). The knowledge-testing-educational complex strikes back. *American Psychologist*, 66-69.

McClelland, D.C. (1973). Testing for competence rather than for intelligence. *American Psychologist*, 28, 1-14.

McClelland, David, Testing for Competencies rather than Intelligence, *American Psychologist* 28, 1, 1973.

Miles R. & Snow, C. (1984, summer,). Designing strategic human resources systems. *Organizational Dynamics*, 36-52.

Moreau, Ron & Mazumdar, S. Reliance, *Newsweek International*, July 17, 2006.

Moser-Wellman, Annette, *The Five Faces of Genius*, Viking, 2001.

Nador, S. (1997, May 19). Making competency programs work: addressing the concerns of employees. *Canadian HR Reporter*, p. 20.

North, Derek (1993). Applying the competencies approach to management: the Employment Service's experience. *European Review of Applied Psychology*, 43(1), 49-52.

Orr, B. (1995, February 27). Manage competencies through the HR system. *Canadian HR Reporter*, p. 8.

Page, C. (1995). The Competency Confusion: Reframing the Concept and Introducing a Process Model. An unpublished paper originating in the Department of Management Systems at Massey University: Albany.

Pandit, Shrinivas, *Exemplary CEOs: Insights on Organisational Transformation*. Tata McGraw-Hill Publishing Co. Ltd., New Delhi, 2005.

Pandit, Shrinivas, *Thought Leaders: The Source Code of Exceptional Managers and Entrepreneurs*. Tata McGraw-Hill Publishing Co. Ltd., New Delhi, 2002.

Personnel Renewal Council, (1996). Competency-Based Approach to Human Resource Management in the Federal Public Service: a concept paper for discussion. This concept paper was distributed to Heads of Personnel in July 1996.

Pfeffer, Jeffrey (1996). When it comes to best practices, why do smart organizations occasionally do dumb things? *Organizational Dynamics*, 25(1). 33-44.

Pindyck, Robert S., and Rubenfeld, Daniel, L. (1976). *Econometric Models and Economic Forecasts*, McGraw-Hill Book Company.

Piramal, Gita, *Business Maharajas*. Penguin Book, New Delhi, 1996

Polanyi, Michael (1966). *The Tacit Dimension*. Garden City, N.Y.: Doubleday.

Sanghvi, Vir, *Men of Steel: India's Business Leaders in Candid Conversation with Vir Sanghvi*, Lotus Collection, Roli Books, New Delhi, 2007.

Shenoy, P. D., *Strikes – How to Avoid them*. Sterling Publishers Pvt Ltd. New Delhi 1997.

Sherwood, F. P. (1967). Responding to decline in public service professionalism. *Public Administration Review*, 57(3), 211-217.

Sinha, Jai B.P., *The Cultural Context of Leadership and Power*, Sage Publications, New Delhi, 1995.

Snell, Scott & Youndt, Mark (1995). Human resource management and firm performance: Testing a contingency model of executive controls. *Journal of Management*, 21(4), 711-737.

Snow, Charles & Snell, Scott (1993). Staffing as strategy. In Schmitt, Neal, and Borman (eds), *Personnel Selection in Organizations*. San Francisco: Jossey-Bass.

Sternberg, R., Wagner, R., Williams, W. & Horvath, J. (1995). Testing common sense. *American Psychologist*, 50 (11), 912-927.

Suedfeld, Peter (1992). Cognitive managers and their critics. *Political Psychology*, 13, 435-453.

Thakkar, Pradip Mumbai's Amazing Dabbawala, Nov 11, 2005 Rediff.com

Trainor, N. L. (1997, March 10). Five levels of competency. *Canadian HR Reporter*, 12-13.

Winter, N. (1996, April 22). Competencies help create new culture – Bell Sygma's core competencies affect employee selection, advancement, training, performance, management and compensation. *Canadian HR Reporter*, p. 6.

Zemke, R. (1982). Job competencies: can they help you design better training? *Training*, Vol 19 (5), 28-31.

Websites:

http://www.icmr.icfai.org
http://www.straightfromthegut.com/meet/meet_qa.html
www.thocp.net/companies/hewlett_packard/hp_company.htm
http://www.businessworldindia.com/jan2405/index.asp
http://en.wikipedia.org/wiki/Kiran_Mazumdar-Shaw
http://ibef.org/artdisplay.aspx?cat_id=391&art_id=2608
http://www.ciol.com/content/news/2005/105111204.asp
http://www.india-seminar.com/2000/485/485%20interview.htm
http://www.pbs.org/wgbh/commandingheights/shared/minitextlo/int_narayanamurthy.html
http://www.businessweek.com/1998/23/b3581001.htm

http://en.wikipedia.org/wiki/Jack_Welch
http://www.valuebasedmanagement.net/leaders_welch.html
http://www.jackwelchwinning.com/
http://www.infosys.com/about/narayana_murthy.asp
http://en.wikipedia.org/wiki/N.R._Narayana_Murthy
http://www.tata.com/0_media/features/interviews/20001216_mashelkar_1.htm
http://en.wikipedia.org/wiki/Amway
http://www.asiacase.com/ecatalog/NO_FILTERS/page-PROMOTE-539590.html
http://en.wikipedia.org/wiki/Jacques_Nasser
http://www.usnews.com/usnews/biztech/articles/040607/7eewhere.htm
http://www.india-seminar.com/2003/521 521 % 20 paranjoy % 20 guha%20thakurta.htm
http://en.wikipedia.org/wiki/Dhirubhai_Ambani
http://www.hinduonnet.com/thehindu/biz/2002/07/15/stories/2002071500050200.htm
http://www.domain-b.com/management/general/20050430_impossible.html
http://www.hinduonnet.com/fline/fl1503/15030840.htm
http://en.wikipedia.org/wiki/Nokia
http://dhirubhai-ambani-entrepreneur.thejags.info/
http://www.relianceinfo.com/Infocomm/html/media/reliance_drindia_mediakit.html
http://www.adityabirla.com/the_group/speeches.htm
http://www.microsoft.com/events/executives/webcasts.mspx
http://en.wikipedia.org/wiki/Bill_Gates
http://news.com.com/Gates+taking+a+seat+in+your+den/2008-1041_3-5514121.html
http://www.famous-india.com/people-in-india